Lions

# One Foot on the Ground

I can do it, I can do it, Moth told herself.
I've always been able to do pirouettes before.
Madame was beside her, urging her on.
Moth whirled away, determined to escape.

"You are angry. I can see it in your eyes.
You should get angry more often. It makes
you dance better."

Moth blushed and felt furious. Madame
was making fun of her. To her horror, she
felt her eyes brim with tears. She wanted to
go away and hide.

Also available in Lions

# One Foot on the Ground

## Jean Richardson

Illustrated by
Julia Pearson

Lions
*An Imprint of* HarperCollins*Publishers*

First published in Great Britain by Knight Books in 1982
First published by Lions in 1994
1 3 5 7 9 10 8 6 4 2

Lions is an imprint of HarperCollins Children's Books,
a division of HarperCollins Publishers Ltd,
77-85 Fulham Palace Road,
Hammersmith, London W6 8JB

Revised edition text copyright © Jean Richardson 1994
Illustrations copyright © Julia Pearson 1994

ISBN 0 00 674664 0

The author asserts the moral right to be
identified as the author of the work.

Printed and bound in Great Britain by
HarperCollins  Manufacturing Ltd, Glasgow

# 1

## *Madame*

It was more like a performance than a class, but the audience was sitting on the stage. Mothers, sisters, aunts and what were surely grandmothers had arrived early to make sure of seats in the front row, and one or two were now knitting while they waited.

Below them, the class was drawn up in lines, like a regiment about to be inspected. Temporary barres, anchored by weights, ruled off each line, and here and there the more impatient students flexed their muscles in a trial *plié*. Everyone came swiftly to attention as the director and his guest entered.

'Ladies and gentlemen,' – the pianist was the only full-grown gentleman in sight – 'I am delighted and proud to introduce to you the world-famous prima ballerina, Tamara Sherepina. We are honoured that she has consented to teach at this year's summer school, and I'm sure you will all learn a lot from her.'

There was applause as the director raised Sherepina's hand to his lips and his secretary came forward with an armful of flowers.

Moth moved sideways so that she could get a better view of Sherepina. She knew all about her: she'd been given her biography as a birthday present, and the book was upstairs in her room, waiting for a suitable moment to ask Madame to autograph it.

Sherepina had done all the things Moth longed to do, in a long-ago world when it had been possible to be one of the stars of a company at Moth's age. Younger, actually, for she'd been only thirteen when she joined the company, and Moth was fifteen. Hers had been an exciting, demanding world. Dancers had worked long hours and put up with impossible conditions. They'd been herded across Europe by train; they'd rehearsed new productions into the early hours of the morning – after giving an evening performance; they'd danced on sloping stages, slippery stages, stages bristling with splinters and, on one occasion, according to Madame's book, they'd been reduced to doing their class in a field alongside the railway line, using the wire fencing as a barre.

But Sherepina hadn't minded. She had

inspired choreographers to create new roles for her, and she had danced all the classic roles: Giselle, Aurora, Odette-Odile. She had appeared in Monte Carlo, Paris, London, New York, partnered by Massine, Balanchine, Lichine, Dolin – names that belonged to the history of ballet. Now she was too old to dance with anyone, but she handed on her experience at master classes all over the world.

Moth knew that this was how the traditions of ballet were kept alive. History books were for the audience. What dancers needed was personal contact, to hear and above all see how it was done. Sherepina and the other teachers at the summer school were stars who in turn had learned from other stars, in a chain that stretched back to Russia and the Imperial Ballet, and Moth wanted to be a part of that chain. When she discovered that Sherepina was teaching in England during the holidays, she knew that she had to be there,

She could only afford to come to the summer school for a week, and even that was difficult. She couldn't get a grant, and her parents pointed out that it was time her brother Toby had some extras and he wanted to go on a school trip abroad. They couldn't manage both.

In the end, it was Great-Aunt Marion who once again came to Moth's rescue. Her father was concerned that Moth shouldn't take financial help for granted, but her great-aunt only laughed and said: 'I can't take it with me, David, and I'd rather spend the money myself than have the government do it for me.'

The Sherepina of Moth's book was an enchanting ethereal dancer. Moth had looked at the photographs of her so often that she thought she would have recognised her anywhere. But she didn't.

The woman the director introduced was a stranger. She was small and slight and her legs were painfully thin. Her most striking feature was a mane of waved, very blonde hair – but she's dark, Moth thought in dismay – and even at a distance Moth could see she was heavily made-up, with a fake tan and pencilled eyebrows. There was no trace of the wistful charm of the photographs.

Knees bent obediently into *pliés* as they began the familiar routine of class: *pliés, tendus, battements, fondus*. Moth had been doing these movements since she was a small child, but Madame made her feel oddly nervous. The barres creaked and there was a whisper of feet across the floor as the dancers changed position. Madame walked up and down the rows, clapping the beat and correcting any misplaced limbs with an accusing slap.

'You must be conscious of the correct movement,' she said. 'It won't come by magic. You need to be sure that your feet are in exactly the right position.' Her voice was harsh and husky. It jabbed like a splinter.

She talks as though we were just beginning, thought Moth, disappointed. She had expected the insight of a great dancer, not some elementary detail that sounded just like Miss Pearson. *She* had told them to fit their heels neatly into the hollow of their ankles when doing *battements*.

Now it was time for centre practice. Madame was not impressed by their *port de bras*. Her biographer had made much of Sherepina's beautiful arms, and when she raised them in an arc, they cut a shape in the air that had purpose and meaning – unlike the arms around Moth, which wavered uncertainly.

'The meaning must come right through your arms and go out of your nails and on up. When you reach up, you must think up too. Listen to the music. It tells you that your arms are unfolding, and you must imitate the music. It is not jerky, so why are you?'

But it was their *pirouettes* that really roused Madame.

'It is not just a question of the right movement. You must also dance. You must be artists.

Your job is to make the audience forget their troubles. That is what Pavlova said. But you are all so feeble. Why?'

The girls nearest her looked down, embarrassed. They weren't sure whether she expected an answer.

'You must attack: dancing, life, everything. See.' And Sherepina spun across the room. Moth hadn't time to analyse her movements: they exploded in a firework of speed, energy and precision. There was a burst of applause. Even the grandmothers were impressed.

One by one the class tried to copy her. The music was like a wave, carrying each of them forward, and Moth waited for it to lift her off.

'No, no.' Madame stopped her. 'You have no sense of direction. Where are you going? To that corner? OK. Make us feel it.'

Moth began again.

'No, no. You must make a line. All dancing is about lines. Start again.'

Moth returned to the corner. The others had retreated to the sides of the floor, leaving a wide open space. She could sense their dread of being singled out in the same way. The women on the platform were enjoying the tension: thank goodness she wasn't their daughter!

I can do it, I can do it, Moth told herself. I've always been able to do *pirouettes* before. Now

Madame was beside her, urging her on. The beautiful arms had veined hands with scarlet nails. It was like a race, with Madame always at her side. Moth whirled away, determined to escape.

'Better, better. Now you are feeling something. You are angry, I can see it in your eyes. You should get angry more often. It makes you dance much better.'

Moth blushed and felt furious. Madame was making fun of her. Why couldn't she stick to sensible comments, like Miss Pearson. The words were English, but the feeling behind them was foreign. Moth was aware of an alien temperament and culture to which she didn't have the key. She wasn't sure what she had expected of Madame, but she hadn't foreseen this. To her horror, she felt her eyes brim with tears. She wanted to go away and hide.

She wasn't sure whether Madame noticed. Perhaps the lecture was over, anyway. The procession of *pirouettes* resumed. Many of the others were far worse than Moth but Madame let them go, contenting herself with shouting every now and then, 'Aim for the corner.'

When the class ended, everyone clapped and Madame was immediately surrounded by autograph hunters. They waved albums, photographs, books on ballet, odd scraps of paper, and Madame signed everything, patting the smallest children on the head.

Moth made for her holdall, which was underneath a mountain of sweaters and track suits. One or two girls glanced at her, but nobody said anything and she pretended to be absorbed in changing her shoes. When she looked up, she thought Madame made a gesture in her direction, as though she wanted to speak to her, but Moth looked away. There was nothing she wanted to say to Madame – and she certainly didn't want her autograph. She remembered how she had badgered them all to let her come – because of Madame. Now, after only one class, she bitterly regretted having made such a fuss. If only her great-aunt had not been so obliging. If only she hadn't been able to come.

# 2

## *'I'm a dancer . . .'*

The cattle-grid at the entrance to the drive was designed to keep out the sheep who came down from the moors in search of grass. Moth was surprised how bold and determined they were, though as soon as she tried to get near any of them, they turned tail and skipped nimbly away. She wanted to feel their coats, though they looked discouragingly matted with mud, but she had to be content with the wisps of wool scattered about, which had a comforting softness.

She wasn't sure whether there were any rules about leaving the college grounds, but what did it matter? At the worst they could only ask her to go, and that was what she wanted to do.

The college was right on the edge of the town, and the moors – here a mass of dense bracken and mauve heather – rose steeply on the other side of the road. There was a network of paths no wider than a footprint, and Moth took one that seemed as if it would lead to a little clearing halfway up the hillside. Around her was the clatter of falling water, and she saw that it was trickling down a scar in the rocks, gathering speed as it raced over a chain of boulders and dropped suddenly out of sight.

The open, empty countryside made her faintly uneasy. She was used to the familiar streets of her home town, or the part of London where she lived with her great-aunt and cousin Libby during term time. Her great-aunt was always warning them of the dangers of London – traffic, strangers, motorbikes, being out alone after dark – but her fears were at least human-size. Here Moth felt overwhelmed by the vast scale of the scenery, by an expanse of sky and landscape against which she was tiny.

She was relieved when she got to the clearing and found she could still see the college. It was familiar if not beautiful; from above, the modern extension looked like a heap of cardboard boxes that had been carelessly chucked out of the back door of the grey stone main building.

Moth sat down on the weathered plank of a seat and wished she had someone to talk to. She didn't know anyone else on the course, and it was the first time she'd been away entirely by herself. She thought back to her first days at the

Fortune School, when her great-aunt had seemed so remote and formal and Moth had wanted to run home and tell her mother about Marina, the school's star pupil, who had shouted at Moth for interrupting her practice. Marina had achieved Moth's dearest ambition – a place at the Upper School of the Royal Ballet – and was now a member of the company.

She found herself half-wishing that Libby had come on the course instead of going home to Australia. Cousin Libby wouldn't have been upset by Sherepina, whatever she'd said, and she would have got to know everyone.

Moth wasn't like that. She had always been shy. Sometimes she wished that she had Libby's extrovert nature, that she was what her great-aunt called 'a good mixer'. But although she knew that people often thought she was stuck-up, her friendships, once made, were lasting, whereas Libby kept on the outside of people and didn't bother to know anyone really well.

It was disconcerting being up here with only the sheep for company. They tended to bob up among the bracken, stare curiously at Moth, decide that she was harmless, and resume their nibbling. It was so quiet she could hear them tearing the stems from the ground, and they ate continuously and hastily, as though they hadn't a moment to lose.

The college was like that, too. All bustle. Students consulted noticeboards, checked lists, compiled timetables. There were lectures, films, demonstrations by dancers from the Royal Ballet. It was up to the students to find out for themselves when and where they were. The prospectus had made it sound so inviting, a step into a wider, more adult world. And now Madame had spoiled it all.

Moth tried to work out why she had minded so much. She had often been criticised and corrected, but it was different at the Fortune. Classes were small, she knew everyone, and she was used to Miss Pearson's sarcasm. No one here knew anything about her. She had to make her own way among students from all over the country. There was no one to say, 'Yes, Moth Graham was off form today, but she's one of our most promising pupils.'

Here the only thing that would single her out was talent. The onlookers, if they knew anything about dancing, would pick her out because of an elusive quality called line. Moth found it difficult to define, but she was beginning to recognise it in others. It was to do with the way you carried your head and placed your limbs so as to create a shape that was instinctively pleasing. It was bound up with ease and confidence, for dancing wasn't just a physical skill. It said something

13

about all of you, about the things you knew you
could do and the things you were afraid of. If
you persevered and got the right teaching, you
could probably master the technical problems,
but you also needed courage and determination
to cope with criticism, competition, injuries and
disappointments. Looked at like that, Moth
wasn't so sure that she still wanted to be a
dancer.

She had forgotten to put on her watch and
had no idea of the time. It must surely be
lunchtime by now. If she was going on with the
course, she would have to have lunch and get
ready for the afternoon class with Madame. She
wasn't any longer one of the crowd, but the girl
who Madame had reduced to tears. And if she
picks on me, Moth thought, it could happen
again. I cry so easily, even when I don't want to.

The indecisive sun, which had been in and out
all morning, suddenly flooded the hills with a
wash of yellow light. Moth watched the path of
a racing cloud mirrored in a patch of darting
shadow. Below her, families – tempted at last to
picnic in the open – tumbled out of a row of
parked cars. A child ran up the path towards
her.

She was about nine, the same age as Moth's
younger sister, but unlike Lyn, who shared
Moth's ordinary brown colouring, this girl had

auburn ringlets and the air of a child who knows she is pretty. She certainly wasn't shy, for she came over to Moth and asked inquisitively: 'What are you doing up here?'

Moth tried to think of a smart answer, but she wasn't in the right mood and ended up saying tamely, 'I'm thinking. What are you doing?'

'We're having a picnic,' said the child, adding, 'we're on holiday, my mummy and daddy and my sister,' and to confirm this, the rest of the family arrived.

'It's a fair pull up that hill,' said the woman, collapsing thankfully on to the seat beside Moth. 'You don't mind if we sit here, do you?'

'Of course not, I'm just going, anyway.' Moth got up.

'Live round here, do you?' asked the woman curiously. 'It's a lovely part, isn't it?'

'I'm a stranger, too,' Moth explained. 'I'm just here for a few days, doing a course at the college. I'm a dancer,' she added.

She hadn't expected them to be impressed, but they were. 'Do you hear that, Carmen?' said the woman. 'This young lady's a dancer. That's what you want to be, isn't it?'

The auburn ringlets nodded. Carmen seemed to have lost her tongue.

'Have you danced in public at all?' asked the woman.

'Yes. I've been in *The Nutcracker* and several other productions in London.'

'You must be very good. You're lucky to be good at something. I keep telling Carmen, it must be a wonderful life if you've got talent. So satisfying too, doing something creative. Only wish I'd had the chance.'

'Yes, it is.' And Moth suddenly knew that it was, that the chance of becoming a dancer was worth any number of scenes with Madame. How could she ever have thought otherwise?

'We'll look out for you,' said the woman. 'Perhaps one of these days we shall see you on the box.'

'Perhaps. And I hope Carmen does well too, then she can come to the summer school here and learn from real dancers.'

Carmen had been doing an exhibition dance complete with *pirouettes*, but her sister barged into her and the two little girls rolled over on to the grass. Moth could hear familiar squeals as she ran down the hill, and she was glad to be reminded of Toby and Lyn. She would see them at the end of the week and, in the meantime, she had to get on with the business of becoming a dancer – even at the cost of another scene with Madame.

# 3

## New Worlds

'Gruelling, wasn't it?'

The girl who spoke looked exhausted. She was wearing a pale washed-out blue leotard, and wisps of curl had strayed from her bun.

Moth nodded. She'd helped herself to far too much salad and felt obliged to finish it, which involved chewing as tirelessly as a sheep.

'Did you see her next class?'

Moth shook her head.

'It was a hoot. You know that enormous fat woman who's always on the platform watching over her little darling. The child's got everything – hundreds of pairs of shoes and a different leotard for every class – but she can't dance for toffee. Mother's the one who wants to dance, and she's determined to make dear Deborah do it for her. Madame didn't know what she was taking on. They were doing attitudes, and

17

Madame got hold of Deborah's leg and twisted it right back. The child burst into tears, and her mother was furious. She swelled up like a balloon, and I thought she was going to take off from the platform and flatten Madame.'

'What happened?' Moth's voice was muffled by her salad.

'Well, as soon as Deborah started crying, Madame was horrified. She flung her arms round her and started kissing her. Deborah was terrified, and Madame spent the rest of the class being very protective. She kept asking Deborah whether she was all right and giving her special attention, when all the poor kid wanted was to merge into the background and be inconspicuous.'

'I hope she won't take any more notice of me.' Moth was alarmed at the thought of being kissed. 'It's someone else's turn for special attention.'

'As long as it's not me.' The girl caught up a tendril of hair and skewered it firmly with a hairpin. 'I only dance a couple of times a week, and I'm not used to this pace. Our group is really too advanced for me. Some of them are at the Royal Ballet School.'

'Which ones?' Moth wanted to identify her future rivals.

'There's a little group of them who were here

last week as well. Wait till we have to do *jetés*.
One boy can leap halfway across the room. And
make sure you don't stand behind him at the
barre. He does his *battements* as though his legs
were joined on by elastic.'

By now Moth was almost looking forward to
the afternoon class. She found a place halfway
along the barre, where she was screened by a
taller girl. She was almost opposite the wonder
boy, whose pale skin went with hair the colour
of a fox. Moth dubbed him the 'Blue Boy',
because he was wearing a shiny kingfisher-blue
body-stocking. She noticed there was even
something distinctive about the gentle *pliés* with
which he was warming up.

Madame was as relentless as ever, but this time
she stayed at the front of the class. Feeling she
was safely out of sight, Moth began to relax – if
that was the right word for intense concentration
and effort. As she watched Sherepina, she began
to appreciate movements and gestures that had
been perfected over a lifetime.

Sherepina was made up of beautiful lines. Her
head and arms moved as though they were
bounded by an invisible circle that enclosed her.
And yet, Moth thought, although her movements are so ordered, they don't look at all
mechanical. It's as though her head just happens
to be in the right place.

They did a sequence that ended in an *arabesque*. The Blue Boy's legs were like the arms of a clock. He fixed them effortlessly in space, one supporting him while the other stretched out to match the line of his arm. Everyone clapped his *jetés*. He soared across the room, striding through the air and smiling as though slightly surprised when he landed. Moth forgot herself in the excitement of trying to learn from far better dancers.

Madame had to be reminded when it was time to stop. The grannies and aunties wanted their tea, but for Madame it was an annoying distraction. Moth didn't want to stop either. She was experiencing the happiness of a good class, when everything goes well and technical worries suddenly solve themselves, like a troublesome key finally turning in a lock. But they had to make way for the dance demonstration that was to be held that evening.

It had the atmosphere of a gala performance. Moth was glad that her mother had insisted on her bringing a flowered skirt along with her jeans, for it was plainly an occasion for dressing up. She wore her long hair loose, held back with slides, outlined her eyes lightly with eyeliner and got out the silver gipsy earrings that she had been given by her great-aunt.

'You'll lose them,' her mother had warned,

reminding her that they were real silver and quite valuable, but Moth took no notice. What was the point of having such unusual earrings if they were too precious to wear!

She was glad that she'd made an effort to look her best, because everyone was transformed. Even the scruffy pianist had put on a dark suit and a tie, and the eleven-year-olds, darting around like impatient tadpoles, had pretty dresses and ribboned manes of well-brushed hair. The front rows of the audience seemed to be made up of grey-haired ladies with set curls still warm from the hair-dryer.

Moth and her new friend, whose name was Alison, found seats behind the indignant fat mother, who had a Jack Sprat of a husband, a thin little man who was obviously used to doing as he was told. Deborah, adorned with outsize hair-ribbons, was clutching an expensive history of the Royal Ballet and had been made to find out all about who was dancing.

The centre of the front row was reserved. 'Special guests,' whispered Alison as the director, looking suitably theatrical in a grey velvet jacket and a mauve frilled shirt, led them in.

Sherepina looked magnificent. She wore a simple black dress, and diamonds sparkled beneath the blonde waves and on her fingers.

One ring had a glittering stone the size of an egg laid by the Firebird.

Alison identified the other guests. 'The one in the peacock dress teaches at White Lodge. The pretty young one comes from the Danish Ballet, the man with glasses is a ballet critic, and the guest of honour is a famous dancer who's even older than Sherepina. Don't they look funny kissing.'

The two retired ballerinas greeted each other as though they were centre stage. Even their kisses had a hint of rivalry, and they were careful to sit one each side of the director.

The programme opened with a *pas de deux* from one of Moth's favourite ballets, Macmillan's *Romeo and Juliet*, which her great-aunt had taken her to see. The dancers used the body of the hall as a stage, and danced right up to the encircling rows of chairs. For once they were not disguised by distance, and Moth could see the sweat running down Romeo's face and the movement of his muscles as he lifted Juliet. She loved his reddish-gold curls and the feeling of a live, visibly breathing dancer, but some of the elderly ladies were plainly not used to having such a virile young man virtually in their laps.

The dancers wore practice dress, and its plainness concentrated attention on the quality of the dancing. There were cheers for the Blue Bird solo from *The Sleeping Beauty* with its challenging jumps, but Moth preferred the Blue Boy in class. He had flown so naturally across the room, whereas this boy was showing off his technique.

The girl in the final *pas de deux* wore a tatty gauze skirt that was about as romantic as an old corset, but emphasised her fragile beauty. Moth felt as though in some way she had conjured her up, for it was Marina, the former star of the Fortune School. She looked as aloof as ever, and didn't seem at all surprised by the burst of clapping in tribute to her *fouettés*.

'I know her,' Moth whispered to Alison. 'She used to be at our school.' She would like to have spoken to Marina, but as soon as the applause came to an end the dancers were swamped by a wave of autograph hunters led by Deborah, who had been pushed forward by her mother and was struggling to get her giant history of the Royal Ballet open at the right page. Marina scribbled a few gracious signatures before the director hustled the dancers away, dismissing their fans with: 'We don't want them to miss their train. They've all got a performance tomorrow.'

The distant aura of Covent Garden lingered in the corridors. The display had been as brief and dazzling as fireworks, and no one wanted to come down to earth. There was talk of other performances, of bringing more companies to the north, or arranging trips to London. Dancing had worked its heady magic on parents, teachers and pupils, for whom it was often no more than a weekly session of routine exercises in a classroom. Now they saw where it could lead . . .

'What do we do now?' asked Moth, feeling that the evening had only just begun.

'You can come up to my room if you like,' said Alison. 'It's what we did last week. We got some Coke from the dining room and then everyone talked.'

Everyone turned out to be most of the girls in Alison's corridor. They crowded into her room, finding a space on the beds, the chairs, the floor, and they talked. About the teachers here and those at home, about what was wrong and what they would have liked instead, about themselves and what they were hoping to do.

Moth found herself doing an imitation of Madame. 'You must work like hell,' she said, copying Madame's stance and turning her feet out at an absurd angle. She caught Sherepina's cosmopolitan accent – a cocktail of American, Russian and French – and began correcting the positions of the girls lounging round her. She had an instinct for the tricks of speech and movements that characterise people, and she had

24

learned at school that making people laugh was a useful disguise for shyness. She had once reduced a class to helpless laughter by mimicking one teacher's pronunciation, so that the poor woman was unable to read out the dullest fact without everyone giggling. Her mother said it was unkind and would get her into trouble one day, but Moth, who didn't mean to be hurtful, couldn't resist a likely subject.

Now, having made everyone laugh, she was one of the group and could relax and listen. She was back in a world she had left behind when she went to the Fortune School, the world of girls who went to classes in the evenings and on Saturdays, who competed at festivals, who thought of dancing in terms of their local teacher, and who wanted to be teachers themselves. They talked of courses at colleges, summer schools and dance centres, of dancing at discos and workshops, of jazz and modern dance. Dancing to them didn't mean the far-off splendour of Covent Garden, but half a dozen dancers doing a show at the local arts centre.

Their talk gave Moth a new view of dancing, and although she clung to her childhood vision of being on *pointes* in a white filmy dress – drifting across the stage, perhaps, as Giselle – she responded to the quite different ambitions of those around her. When I'm a real student, she thought, when at last someone looked at her watch and they all stole hastily off to bed, it will be like this all the time. And the thought of all the dancing and talking that lay ahead was wonderfully exciting.

# 4

## *More Madame*

The rest of the week was brimming with activity.
Moth had never practised so much. A class all
the morning, a class all the afternoon, and always
in the background the sounds and smell of
dancing: tinkling pianos, sweat, feet thudding,
voices hastening from one studio to the next.
She felt caught up in a machine that bruised and
hustled her and made her question whether she
really wanted a life like this.

Alison was sure she didn't. 'I'm just not good
enough,' she confessed to Moth, as they were
returning from a class in one of the outlying
studios. 'I haven't got the patience to do a
movement again and again until it's perfect. I
adored dancing when I was little. I was so proud
of my ballet shoes, and I used to put them on at
home and dance round to a record of *Swan
Lake*. My idea of heaven was to have a class

every day, and I wouldn't have believed that I could ever get tired of it. But I have. I know now that I'll never be good enough. I shall go on dancing for fun, but I could never be really dedicated. I just don't care about it that much.'

A chill wind tugged at them as they made for the shelter of the main building. Moth dodged a puddle and felt sad for Alison. 'I don't feel like that,' she said, 'but I'm not sure whether I'm good enough. I've been watching the Blue Boy, and I can see how good he is. It's not just his fantastic jumps. There's another boy who jumps just as high, but you don't *have* to watch him. It's making people feel they can't take their eyes off you that counts.'

Moth would like to have talked to the White Lodge group, but they kept themselves apart. She noticed that they were on easy terms with all the teachers, who were plainly impressed by the Blue Boy. One day she managed to get a place at their table in the dining room and learned that the Blue Boy, who was older than he looked, was at the Upper School and had just been offered a place in the company.

'Back row of the chorus for you,' said one of the girls teasingly.

The Blue Boy grinned. 'Me and plenty of others,' he said. 'No one gets much of a showing these days – unless there's a crop of injuries.

Everyone grumbles about getting so few chances. Tony was saying that he's done so few performances that it's a nightmare when it's his turn to go on. You'll probably do more dancing as a teacher, Di, than I shall.'

Di shrugged. Moth had admired her neat movements in class, but her full breasts and generous hips were all wrong for a company dancer. 'I'd still rather be in the company,' she said.

They've only exchanged one lot of problems for another, thought Moth. Libby and I compete as the best in our class, but there are lots of other schools and hundreds more classes. Even if I do get to the Upper School, far from being over, the competition will become more fierce and frightening.

Madame was now teaching the youngest group, and Moth's class had moved on to the Danish teacher, who looked like a young athlete in her grey track suit and scolded them like an older sister. She introduced them to the distinctive style of the Bournonville ballets – such as *La Sylphide* – that she danced in Copenhagen. The name was new to most of the class, though the ballets themselves were more than a hundred years old.

Moth hadn't yet asked Sherepina to sign the copy of her biography, although after several marvellous classes she'd become one of Madame's greatest fans. Whenever she had the book with her, Madame always seemed to be besieged by admirers, and Moth didn't want to be one of a jostling crowd. But she had still not managed to catch Madame on her own, when she heard that Sherepina was leaving the next day, immediately after class, to fly on to another engagement.

Although Moth knew where Madame's room was, she wasn't sure that she ought to disturb her. Supposing she resented such an intrusion? She might be resting, or even asleep. Moth dreaded an irate reception, but it was a chance she had to take if she wanted Madame's autograph.

After supper she slipped up to Sherepina's room and knocked on the door. There was no reply. Moth came back three times, but there was still no reply. Madame must have gone out for a farewell dinner.

I'll just have to wait until she comes back, Moth thought, even if it means sitting up until midnight. She didn't want to tell her room-mate what she was doing, so she got undressed and pretended to go to bed. Around eleven o'clock she crept out again, hoping the girl wouldn't wake up and wonder where she'd gone.

Madame was still not back, and Moth felt awkward standing around in her nightdress.

Halfway along the corridor was a little alcove with an old chintz armchair in it. It was a relic of the days when the college had been a spa hotel, where guests came to drink the water from a spring up on the moors. The spring was still there, but the fashion for drinking from it had passed.

Moth knelt on the chair and looked out of the window. The view was a series of dots of light that reminded her of the puzzles she had loved as a child. If I joined them all up, she thought, there would be shops, houses, a church, the outline of a small town. As her eyes got used to the darkness, she could distinguish shades of blackness beneath a cloud-spotted moon. It was like looking at a photographic negative and trying to guess the scene.

From time to time within the building doors opened and shut, but no one appeared. Moth felt as though she was dreaming. She was frightened of falling asleep – if she hadn't done so already – and so she began to practise a few steps. The corridor made an inviting if narrow stage, and she imagined that she was Juliet, waiting for Romeo.

She was reaching out yearningly towards Madame's door in a perfect *arabesque* when she heard footsteps. Madame hastened towards her, preceded by a wave of heavy perfume. Moth felt shy and foolish.

'Is something wrong? Are you ill?'

'Oh, no. I'm sorry to bother you,' – how ridiculous it now seemed to be hanging around in the middle of the night – 'but I wanted to ask you if you could autograph this for me.' Moth picked up the book which she had left outside Madame's door. 'I didn't have a chance to ask you in class and . . .' she faltered. Madame was looking stern. 'And I won't have a chance to see you tomorrow, as I have a class when you're leaving.' The last part came out in a rush.

'You have been waiting here for me to come back? How long?'

'I don't know. I think it was about eleven when I came up.'

'*Mon Dieu!* It is past midnight now. We must not stand around in the corridor. We might wake someone up. You should be in bed. Come into my room for a minute while I sign your book.'

It was a student's room, like Moth's, but there were clothes everywhere and the dressing-table was littered with make-up, as though Madame had got ready for a performance. She was used to having a dresser to tidy up after her. The bouquet that had begun the week was drooping

a little now, but the perfume that filled the room
came from something more exotic than a vase of
English flowers. More than anything else in the
room, it suggested to Moth another – foreign –
world.

'You are keen to dance?'

'Oh yes, more than anything in the world.'

Sherepina looked at Moth intently. Her eyes
were magnified by shadow and liner, and her
lashes swept up in a stiff fringe. 'Aren't you the
girl I scolded about her *pirouettes*?'

'Yes, Madame.'

'Well, if you want to be a dancer, you must
learn to take criticism. You will be shouted at
many times – and by people far more fierce than
I. Can you take it? Are you tough enough?'

'I don't know,' Moth confessed. 'But I want
to try.'

'Good. You are so spoiled, you little English
girls. You have nice kind parents and nice kind
teachers and you think it is all so easy. But
dancing is a terrible life. One part pleasure, nine
parts hard work. And full of disappointments.
You think I am exaggerating, trying to put you
off, but if you go on, you will see that what I
say is true. What is your name?'

'Moth Graham.'

'Moth? That is a strange name – but good for
a dancer.'

'It's a nickname,' Moth explained. 'My proper name is Jennifer, but I've always been called Moth.'

'If you dance, it must be Moth. Already it suggests flying through the air. Do you go to a dancing school?'

'Yes, the Fortune School. And I'm hoping to get into the Upper School of the Royal Ballet next year.'

'Good. Well, I wish you luck. And now I must write in this book for you.' Sherepina pushed aside the jumble of crayons and tissues and rested the book on the dressing-table. She wrote rapidly in a large flamboyant hand.

'Now you must go to bed, and I must do my packing.' She looked impatiently at the disorder, and Moth pictured her sweeping it unsorted into a suitcase. '*Bonne chance, ma petite.*' She kissed Moth on both cheeks and the gesture seemed right: affectionate, theatrical, foreign.

As she walked back to her room, Moth looked to see what Sherepina had written. The words danced across the page:

'Best wishes to Moth. Today you want my autograph – I hope some day I shall want yours. Tamara Sherepina.'

# 5

## *Back to Libby*

It was almost impossible to hear anything Libby said because of the noise. It came from a small cassette player and bounced into every corner of the room, cuffing and shaking the air so violently that the glass animals huddled together on the chest of drawers trembled visibly.

Libby was unpacking. She had dumped her suitcase on the bed and a torrent of beach clothes, some still gritty with sand, streamed on to the floor. What she wanted first – her collection of tapes – was at the bottom of the case, and she flung everything else aside to get at them.

She went back to Australia every summer to stay with her grandparents, who had taken on looking after her when her mother was killed in a car crash. Her father, Moth's Uncle Rex, had often been in London when he was a pilot, but now he was grounded and Libby hadn't seen him for nearly a year. Not that it seemed to worry her. Told that one of the girls had lost her mother and seldom saw her father, an outsider would have picked Moth, for there were no apparent scars on Libby. She had learned not to take anything for granted, and that she had only herself to depend on, and she was a born survivor. She was also, as now, not inclined to consider other people's feelings.

'Gran thought this was great.' Moth guessed rather than heard what Libby said. 'I played it on the beach and got everyone dancing. The sand was just right – firm enough for your feet not to sink in. It made the most fabulous surface. I did some modern dance routines and other people copied me.' She kicked off her trainers and slid her body into the music, which took her on board like a big dipper at a funfair.

Moth stayed sitting on the floor. It wasn't her kind of music. Libby spent hours in music shops, not buying – she didn't have the money for that – but flipping through the racks and persuading the assistants to play her choice. She was friendly with a boy called Evan who worked in a shop near school. He had only just left school himself, and played drums in a group.

Evan told Libby they'd made a tape and were looking for someone to launch it as a single.

Libby wanted to go to one of his gigs, but the group played in clubs and pubs late at night, and she knew it was useless asking her great-aunt if she could go. She even decided, with unusual tact for her, not to wear the acid green T-shirt Evan had given her, in case her great-aunt asked awkward questions. Evan's short spiky hair and gold earring would arouse her worst suspicions, and she would never understand, as Libby did, that he was a serious musician who spent all his waking hours dreaming of a new sound. But then pop music was one of her great-aunt's pet aversions.

'Turn that dreadful noise off.' Not unnaturally, in view of the din, they had not heard Great-Aunt Marion coming up the stairs. She was finding the stairs more difficult these days, and didn't come up to their rooms as often as in the past, but this occasion, it seemed, was an emergency.

'The whole house is shaking. There'll be cracks in the walls and the floor will give way if you carry on like this. These old houses weren't built to stand up to this kind of destructive racket.'

Moth stopped the tape and Libby assumed an expression of innocent surprise. 'Gran loved it,' she said. 'She said it did her good to hear something so full of life. It made her want to dance.'

'Well my dancing days are over, and it just sounds like a lot of noise to me. I used to love dancing, but we had proper tunes in those days with words you could understand, not just the same thing chanted over and over again.'

'That's part of the rhythm,' Libby explained, though she knew it was a waste of time. 'I don't know how you can keep still.'

'Don't you?' Her great-aunt was being sarcastic. 'Well, at least I've managed to survive with my hearing intact. You two have apparently already damaged yours. I've been calling for ages that supper's nearly ready, but I couldn't make myself heard above that row.'

'Sorry. Shall we come now?' Moth had inherited her mother's gift for peace-making, and secretly sympathised with her great-aunt.

'Supper will be ready in ten minutes. Perhaps one of you could come down and lay the table. You, Moth, while Libby tidies up her things. This room was given a thorough clean while you were away, and that bedspread has just been washed. I suppose you didn't notice when you put that dirty case on it.'

'Thank goodness we'll soon be old enough to live on our own,' said Libby, as soon as her great-aunt was out of earshot.'

'Could we?' It had never occurred to Moth that they might live anywhere else.

'Of course, if we got a flat. There are lots of students looking for somewhere to share, and you and I could share a room. We could come and go whenever we liked, and have all the music we wanted without having to worry about upsetting an old lady.'

'But Gam's been super to us . . .'

'Sure,' Libby agreed impatiently, 'but she's incredibly old and we're young. She wants us to be quiet and tidy and go at her pace, but that's not living. And I want to live.'

Libby shovelled everything back into her suit-case and heaved it off the bed. Moth saw that the edges of the case had scribbled on the bedspread, which now looked grubby and creased. As she went downstairs, she reflected how restless and unsettling Libby was, for it wasn't only neat bedrooms that she could turn upside down.

Later, when she was in bed, Moth found herself thinking over what Libby had said. A flat of their own. But was that what she wanted? She was fond of this room, with its uneven sloping ceiling so characteristic of the attics of old houses. It was the first room she'd had all to herself, and it had grown up with her. She kept her most treasured possessions here – ballet posters, her photographs of dancers, some of them signed, her books, the programmes of all the ballets she'd seen. Here they were safe from Lyn's destructive fingers and her mother's periodic habit of having a good turnout and throwing away all the things Moth most wanted to keep.

Her father had made her a noticeboard on which she pinned up postcards and cuttings to do with dancing. At present, there was an article on a new ballet which she'd found in one of the colour supplements, and this season's brochures for Sadler's Wells and Covent Garden. Moth always helped herself to all the free leaflets in the local library, and her great-aunt obligingly subscribed to a mailing list that sent details of visiting dance companies.

She didn't often get to see the things she read about – unless there were cheap tickets on offer at school – but she liked the feeling that she knew what was going on. At least she'd heard of the Northern Ballet Theatre and the Ballet Rambert, unlike Libby, for whom dancing revolved around herself.

Libby cared little, too, about her surroundings, and would be happy dossing down anywhere, whereas Moth suspected that although her spirit was adventurous, she did mind about having clean sheets and her own things. She knew that any room shared with Libby would be strewn with unwashed tights and discarded shoes, and would probably smell of the same. Libby wouldn't care. Sometimes she borrowed one of Moth's books, and weeks later Moth would rescue it from under the bed, or wherever Libby had happened to abandon it. She was always surprised when Moth got cross.

'It's only a book,' she would say. 'You carry on as though I was ill-treating a person.'

No, thought Moth, surveying her tidy kingdom before she switched off the light, I wouldn't enjoy sharing. Libby can please herself what she does next year, but I'm staying here. I don't want to leave home yet.

# 6

## *An Invitation*

The first few days of term were full of plans for the future. The threat of nearing GCSEs hung over every lesson, parents made appointments to see Miss Lambert, people talked seriously about qualifications, and even familiar events like the end-of-term show assumed a new importance. Moth's week at the summer school rapidly receded into the background.

'A witch,' said Ruth crossly to Moth. 'I've got to be one of the witches in a scene from *Macbeth*, while that awful Juliette has got the part I wanted. You don't think I look like a witch, do you?'

Ruth was becoming increasingly sensitive about her appearance. She was already a younger version of her mother – short, dark and plump – and she was convinced that there were no great roles for short plump actresses. Her great attraction was her voice, which was low and distinctive.

When she read aloud, she coloured words and gave them a texture that emphasised their sound as much as their meaning.

'I wanted to do Viola,' she wailed, not waiting for Moth to answer. 'That scene where she woos Olivia disguised as a page. Juliette may look the part, but she hates Shakespeare and she hasn't a clue. She might just as well be a witch.'

'She'd be hopeless,' said Moth. 'She'd never stoop to creeping round a cauldron; she wants to show off her legs. They're her main asset. She's like Jane. One of life's princesses.'

> ' "When shall we three meet again,
>      In thunder, lightning or in rain?" '

intoned Ruth, who in spite of her complaining couldn't wait to try out the part. 'It's quite fun being a witch actually, and I can do a marvellous make-up, but no one will spot me being a witch. I bet Emma Thompson or Juliet Stevenson' – she was Ruth's current idol – 'never played the third witch.'

'Well, you're going to drama school,' said Moth comfortingly, 'and you'll get better parts there. Not many famous actresses were discovered at your age. They all seem to have gone somewhere like RADA first.'

'The theatre's a lot to do with luck,' said Ruth gloomily. 'Dan's always on about how important it is to have the right person in the audience.'

Daniel, Ruth's older brother, was determined to become a concert pianist, and his ambition came first in the Fisher household. He had private lessons from a distinguished pianist, and practised for so many hours every day that life had to be organised round him.

Moth would love to have heard him play, but she went to the house as Ruth's friend, and she saw that Ruth resented being second to her brother. On the odd occasions when Daniel did appear, he was either silent or off-hand, and Moth didn't know what to say to him.

'He's a pain in the neck at the moment,' said Ruth. 'He's preparing for a recital, and it always makes him irritable. He practises all day and then screams if I want to play a CD. And they're always on his side,' she added, referring to her parents.

'Where's he playing?' Moth had visions of somewhere grand, like the Festival Hall.

'At home. We're going to move the drawing-room furniture round and hire a lot of chairs. It's going to be a party, with wine and fiddly things to eat. Do you want to come?'

'Would Dan invite me?' Moth doubted whether Daniel remembered she existed.

'Course not, silly. *I'm* asking you. It's my house too, and you could help pass things round.

I'm sure Mummy would be glad of an extra pair of hands, and I want someone to talk to.'

'What would I have to wear?' Moth wasn't sure whether she wanted to go to a smart party – well, not in the wrong clothes.

'Anything. Not jeans, or Mummy'll blow a fuse. But a dress, or a skirt and top, would be fine. I'm having a new dress because Mummy's trying to be extra nice to me. Aren't parents obvious! They think I mind about Dan getting all the attention, and buying me a new dress is supposed to make it all right. I bet it won't be the kind of dress I want anyway, but something Mummy likes.'

Moth sympathised. Her parents sometimes wanted her to be someone she wasn't – someone, she felt, they would have preferred as a daughter. She could understand how Ruth felt about Daniel, because although her brother Toby didn't know what he wanted to be, whenever her parents spoke about his future, it always sounded more important than hers.

'I sometimes wish Dan would do something wrong – forget his music, or come out in spots. He's terribly vain, and he takes himself so seriously. He worries for weeks beforehand about getting a cold. I think he'd lock me in my room if he thought I'd got a sore throat. I wonder if you need to be quite so dedicated to be a success?'

'Dancers are,' said Moth. 'I read that Lynn Seymour upset everyone else in the company because she insisted on practising so much.'

'Dan's like that. He plays the same few notes over and over, and then when you hear the whole piece, he's woven them in so that you don't even notice them. People who are really good at things are frightening. They're not human.'

Toby, Moth thought, was all-too human. How often had she envied Ruth a house full of music, and parents who cared about the arts and thought they were worthwhile. She didn't want to change her parents, but she found increasingly that she couldn't share the things she loved with them.

'Very nice,' they'd say, if she got them to listen to a piece of music she thought was really special, but she knew that they were only half-listening and half-thinking about something quite different. She'd noticed this particularly in the recent holidays, when worries about her father's job and the family finances had been like a persistent black cloud. Ruth's parents listened, though it seemed they too didn't really listen to her.

'I'll come to Dan's concert if you're sure it's all right, but could your mother ring up and tell my great-aunt about it. Gam likes invitations to be official.'

'OK.'

One of the first years ran past them and began to ring the bell, shaking it as though she was a town-crier. It was the end of break.

The next lesson was Moth's least favourite: geography. As she began to copy down a map showing the rivers of England, she thought instead about something she hadn't confided even to Ruth.

Miss Pearson had asked her if she would like to devise a ballet for the Christmas show. A ballet of her own, lasting about five minutes, to any music she liked, and involving at least two other people. Moth felt both excited and apprehensive. It was a chance to show what she could do – and the most important person in her life might be in the audience – but it needed a good idea, and ever since Miss P. had spoken to her, her mind had been alarmingly blank.

# 7

## *The Recital*

Mrs Fisher closed the curtains, shutting out the wintry darkness, and looked round the drawing-room. The Steinway was open and Daniel's music, usually scattered across the floor, had been tidied away. She straightened the front row of chairs yet again. Were they perhaps a little too near the piano?

Moth found the rows of empty chairs intimidating. 'Is Dan scared?' she asked Ruth.

'I suppose so. He's in a filthy temper. He flies off the handle at the slightest thing, and he keeps fidgeting about the arrangements. He's convinced that most of the audience will be more interested in having a drink and talking to their friends than listening to him.'

'Nonsense, darling,' interrupted Mrs Fisher. 'Of course Dan's nervous. It's an important occasion for him. Hello, Moth. You're looking very pretty.'

Moth wondered whether she ought to return the compliment. Mrs Fisher was hung with jewels like a Christmas tree, and even her smile looks lacquered. 'Who's coming?' she asked, thinking it might be more polite to show an interest in the occasion.

'Friends, Dan's teacher and some of his colleagues, a music critic who we hope will write something nice about Dan and Sir Robin Hepworth, who organises concerts and might ask Dan to play at one of them.'

'They're old and influential,' said Ruth, 'so they might be useful to Dan. They're all "the right sort of people", which means that they're frightfully dull.'

'That's enough, Ruth. Perhaps you and Moth could help carry some food into the dining room. I think we can put the cold things out now.' Mrs Fisher led the way to the kitchen.

'Try some,' said Ruth, sticking a sliver of carrot into a bowl of pale green dip and helping herself to a handful of nuts.

Moth contented herself with a couple of crisps, which she swallowed hastily. She'd never been to such a formal party and wasn't sure what to do. A man in a white jacket was unpacking boxes of glasses. He didn't look very friendly. Was he one of the family?

'He comes with the glasses,' Ruth explained. 'He opens the bottles and pours out the drinks while we hand round hot sausages and bits of quiche. There's masses to eat. Mummy always over-caters.'

Daniel appeared, looking elegant and unfamiliar in a dark suit. 'You won't make the interval too long, will you, Mum,' he said, tugging at his cuffs. 'I don't want a long break once I've played myself in.'

Moth would like to have wished him luck, but she felt too shy. She hadn't seen Dan for some months and he seemed to have grown older – or was it the suit? Usually he wore cords and an open-necked shirt.

As the guests began to arrive, Moth found herself surrounded by a sea of grey, white and bald heads. Most of the men wore dull sober suits, though Daniel's teacher, in a scarlet shirt and velvet jacket, looked defiantly artistic. His speckled mane and beard reminded her of an ageing, slightly shabby lion. His musical colleagues seemed to resemble their instruments: one was as thin and reedy as an oboe, while the other – a French horn, perhaps – was big and brassy. The music critic, gnarled with arthritis, looked as though he never enjoyed anything, while the distinguished Sir Robin had brought

along a man whose chin turned up towards his nose, making him look like Mr Punch. In contrast, the women were as colourful as exotic birds.

Moth and Ruth sat dutifully at the end of a row. Although she wasn't performing, Moth found herself responding to the expectancy of the audience. The drawing room with its marble fireplace and gilt-framed pictures, the Chinese vase with winter sprays of bone-white honesty and orange Japanese lanterns, the arching black wing of the piano in a pool of light, was a world away from home.

Daniel sat down on the piano stool and adjusted the height as though he'd grown since he last sat on it. He waited for the audience to compose themselves – Moth noticed that several people shut their eyes – before he began to play.

The Steinway had an impressive presence – dark and formal – at such close quarters; even Great-Aunt Marion wouldn't have dared ask it to be a little quieter. Moth glanced at her programme, but the titles of the pieces meant nothing to her, though she'd heard of some of the composers.

Daniel's playing was confident and powerful. Notes flew out like sparks or spray. Great waves built up, until Moth felt she was drowning in sound. The music spun her round and round, making her giddy. Daniel would take a phrase and tease it, hiding it between chords, holding it just out of reach, until finally he brought it back with the added joy of recognition. Moth thought she saw how to find her way in music. You had to jump headlong into the sound, then let it unravel and reveal its pattern.

As soon as the applause began, she and Ruth dashed to the kitchen to ferry hot food to the dining room. Moth edged up to the music critic, hoping to overhear praise of Daniel, but he was discussing some new treatment for arthritis and irritably waved her away. The plates of quiche emptied, and Moth went back for the sausage rolls. No one seemed interested in the music. People smiled, said, 'How delicious', and went on talking about shares and the awful weather and problems with the rate of exchange. Moth wondered whether they'd been thinking about these things while Daniel played. It was impossible to tell what music meant to each of them: presumably everyone got the message they wanted to hear.

'Over here,' called Daniel's teacher, winking at her as he demolished a sausage roll in one bite. 'It's hungry work teaching,' he explained. 'And thirsty, too,' said the French horn, draining his glass and signalling to the waiter. Obviously it wasn't done to mention Daniel.

And then someone did. 'Your brother's a very gifted young man,' said Mr Punch, looking down at Moth as though he was trying to find her level.

'I'm not Ruth,' Moth explained. 'She's over there, if you want to speak to her.'

'No, I'd rather speak to you.' Moth found Mr Punch's smile disconcerting. 'If you're not the young man's sister, are you perhaps his girl-friend? He has excellent taste, if I may say so.'

Moth blushed. She wasn't used to compliments from a man older than her father.

'I'm Ruth's friend,' she said firmly. 'We go to the same school.'

'And are you a musician too? I noticed that you seemed to be enjoying the music very much.'

He'd been watching her! Why? She hadn't thought of herself as being worth looking at.

'No, I'm a dancer – at least, I hope to be.'

'A dancer, eh! Yes, you look like a dancer. Keep that lovely long hair and some day you'll dance Giselle.' Mr Punch looked at her with open admiration.

Moth wasn't sure that she liked it. And yet it was flattering to be paid a compliment – even by someone as old as Mr Punch.

'I'm supposed to hand these round,' she said, using the sausage rolls as an excuse to escape, and she pushed her way over to Ruth.

'That man thought I was you,' she said, pointing him out.

Ruth looked in his direction. 'I think he's something at the BBC. He does programmes about young musicians. I suppose he was impressed by Dan.'

Moth was about to say that he'd been more impressed by her and admired her hair, but she wasn't sure that she wanted Ruth to laugh at him. It had been meant as a compliment.

People began to drift back into the drawing room in response to gentle signals from Dr Fisher. Daniel was out of sight, presumably too strung-up for casual conversation.

He began the second half with a thundering sonata, all baffling chords that barred Moth's way into the music. She concentrated instead on Daniel. Remembering how Mr Punch had thought she was his girlfriend, she examined him critically. His legs are too short, she thought, he would never make a dancer. But she admired his thick, dark hair which had a slight wave, much to Ruth's annoyance. She had inherited her father's obstinate straightness. Moth was also attracted by the intensity with which Daniel played – it matched her own feelings about dancing.

The next item was a complete contrast: a series

of short simple pieces. In one, a growling bass line menaced a wistful little treble tune; another had a gently rocking movement that suggested drifting along in a boat. Moth wanted to hear it again. She thought idly about dancing to it, and suddenly saw that it could be the music for her ballet. The pieces were short; she could put two or three contrasting ones together. She wouldn't need a story – that was too difficult in a very short ballet – but perhaps she could illustrate a colour or a mood. Their titles might give her a clue. Her programme had disappeared, so she would have to ask Daniel what the music was. Her mind raced ahead, and she found herself impatient for him to finish. Her own plans were suddenly the most important thing in the world.

But there were several more pieces and an encore before the recital was over. Daniel was surrounded by people eager to congratulate him. Mrs Fisher's eyes sparkled with tears of relief and pride, and Sir Robin and Mr Punch had gone straight to Dr Fisher.

'Let's get some food and go up to my room,' suggested Ruth. 'No one'll miss us.'

But Moth was reluctant to go. She could explain about the music to Ruth – and ask her to find out its title – but that would be tomorrow, or even in a few days' time. She wanted the answer now, so that she could find out first thing tomorrow if there was a recording of it.

She was also afraid that she might lose confidence in her idea. She wanted to follow it up now, in this room with its aura of success. It was like the game she sometimes played with herself: if I get to the corner before the lights change . . . if I don't see a dog on the way home . . . magical, childish ways of warding off disaster or making something fantastic happen. Now the dare was, if I can ask Daniel tonight, the idea will be a success.

Before she could think what to say to Ruth, Mrs Fisher came up and put her arm round Moth. 'We're going to have a quiet family supper when everyone's gone home. You'll stay, won't you? You've been such a help.' She looked radiant and was obviously longing to have her family round her to celebrate Daniel's success. 'Help Ruth clear away the chairs, and then we can sit round the fire.'

They stacked up the chairs and then rearranged the settee, the armchairs and a large matching cushion which Moth chose as her seat. Dr Fisher joined them with Daniel, who didn't seem at all pleased with himself.

'The Chopin was terrible,' he said. 'I can play it so much better.' He seemed determined to find fault with his performance.

'It sounded all right to me,' said Ruth unsym-
pathetically. 'You do make such a fuss. I bet no
one noticed the odd wrong note.'

'There weren't any wrong notes, stupid. It's
just that the piece didn't feel right. I'm not
interested in what people who don't know a
thing about music think. I know how it should
sound – and I bet Hepworth noticed. And that
man from the BBC. You can't fool anyone who
really knows.'

'I'm afraid it's leftovers,' said Mrs Fisher,
coming in at just the right moment with a trolley
laden with food, 'but there's some soup to start
with.'

Moth was halfway through her soup – chicken
with tiny savoury dumplings – before she felt it
was safe to say anything. She was wary of
Daniel, especially in his present mood, so she
addressed her question to them all.

'What were those little short pieces? I'm looking for some music for a ballet for the Christmas
show, and I wondered . . .'

'Alkan,' said Daniel with his mouth full. 'Is
that what you mean? Describe them.'

'One was rather sad, with a sort of growling
accompaniment.'

'*The Mad Woman by the Sea*?' Despite his
mother's protest, Daniel leapt over to the piano
and began to play. 'I always think the bass is the

waves in the background as the poor mad woman dances along the shore. She starts off very slowly, and then whirls herself into a frenzy. I suppose you could dance to it, but it's a bit short.'

'But I thought I could add to it. Perhaps a happy piece showing the woman before she went mad.'

'That's not a bad idea. Maybe something like this.' He went on playing.

'Who is Alkan? I've never heard of him.'

'Ask my father. He's the one who told me about him.'

Moth turned to Dr Fisher who, she realised, enjoyed playing the schoolmaster.

'Well, he was rather a sad man. He was a contemporary of Chopin and Liszt, and he started life as a brilliant pianist. Then he gave up playing in public and seems to have become a kind of recluse. He wrote a lot of music for the piano, some of it so difficult that even Liszt, who was a virtuoso pianist, couldn't play it. But this doesn't seem to have bothered Alkan. He didn't try to get his music performed, and much of it is now lost. But a few admirers preserved some of his work, and now it's being played again.'

'The thing I always remember about him,' said Daniel, who had suddenly found his appetite and seemed more cheerful, 'is that he was killed by a bookcase.'

'How?' Even Ruth was interested.

'Yes, his life was rather like one of his macabre compositions,' said Dr Fisher. 'Apparently when he was an old man, he was taking down a book from the top shelf when the bookcase fell on top of him and crushed him to death.'

'How awful.' Moth wasn't so sure she wanted to use his music now.

'I don't suppose he minded. He probably didn't know much about it, and there are worse ways to die. But about your ballet. I think you'll have to show us the mad woman on a happier day.'

'Are there any recordings of Alkan?' Moth began to think of the practicalities.

'Yes. But if you can't find the right piece, I'm sure Daniel would tape it for you,' said Dr Fisher.

'Would you?' Moth wouldn't have dared to suggest it.

'Sure. And I'll see if I can find you a good piece to go with it.'

Moth's gratitude spilled over into a smile – and Daniel caught it and smiled back. She was so happy that she didn't notice how quiet Ruth had become.

Dr Fisher drove her home, and when Great-

Aunt Marion asked Moth if she'd enjoyed herself, she couldn't for the moment say more than 'Yes.'

She felt as though she had come back from a long journey. Everything that had happened was locked up inside her, and she couldn't share it. So often, at home, when she'd been full of something – like what happened at the summer school – she had tried to tell her mother, who would say simply: 'Yes, dear. Did they? How nice.' The greatest joys, Moth had learned, couldn't be shared – or if they were, it was like music and books, something that essentially went on inside you. You had to take on trust that other people could feel it too.

She was too excited to fall asleep, and found herself thinking about the mad woman and wondering what had made her so unhappy. The haunting little tune came back to her, and she pictured a background of waves, represented perhaps by simple arm movements, while she danced along the shore.

Suddenly she wasn't sure whether she was on the stage or by the sea. Were those the waves or a *corps de ballet*? They couldn't all be at the Fortune School. And this time when she heard the tune, it wasn't being played by Daniel, but by a full orchestra . . .

# 8

## 'The song of the mad woman'

Moth soon found that putting together a ballet of her own wasn't that easy. One of her first problems was recruiting people to dance in it.

'I want everybody to be in something,' said Miss Pearson, who was arranging the programme. 'Drew, Nigel and Paul are still spare, so take your pick.'

Moth, who had been hoping for Tom, the best dancer in their year, was dismayed.

Drew was a pale lanky boy who had shot up like a bolted lettuce. His height seemed to have taken him by surprise, and he danced like a badly-strung puppet.

Nigel was good looking – and knew it. He saw himself as the potential star of a West End musical, and much preferred tap and modern dance to ballet, which he thought was a waste of time.

Paul, however, took ballet very seriously. He was always practising, and was developing into what Miss Pearson called 'a useful dancer', but he seldom smiled and had no gift for attracting attention.

'Nobody could fall madly in love with Paul,' Moth objected, when Libby suggested that he was the best of the bunch.

By now she had worked out the story of the ballet, and on Miss Pearson's advice had kept it very simple.

It started with the mad woman's song danced by Moth as a solo. It wasn't possible to have a group of waves, because no one wanted to drift around at the back while Moth hogged the limelight, so she had to leave it to the music to suggest a wild and lonely shore – helped, she hoped, by a plain blue backcloth.

The middle section explained why the girl was so distraught. In contrast, its music was a cheerful tune – Dan had spoken of a waltz or a mazurka – and the girl danced with a boy until they were interrupted by another girl. All three of them danced together, and then the boy danced with the second girl and finally went off with her. The ballet ended with a repeat of Moth's mad woman solo.

Moth wanted Libby as the other girl, but Libby wasn't sure. She thought that the ballet sounded rather gloomy and old-fashioned.

'Why don't you choose something modern,' she said, 'instead of something obvious like Chopin. I'd like to do a really lively dance, like in a disco, not have to swan around in the past. We're not up to proper partnering yet anyway, so you can't have lifts or any of the elaborate things they have in real romantic ballets.'

Moth had been thinking about that herself. She wanted to express great sadness and great happiness, but she hadn't the experience to interpret them in complicated steps. She was surprised to find that she had unconsciously been thinking more along the lines of modern dance, using simple direct movements quite unlike the artifice of classical ballet.

'I am using modern dance steps,' she said decisively, 'so it won't be old-fashioned. Modern dance ballets have all kinds of music, from electronic noises to string quartets.'

'Well, I'll think about it.' Libby wasn't prepared to commit herself. 'It depends what else comes up, and whether I like the music. Ask me again when you've decided what it is.'

Deciding on the music involved a session with Daniel, and although Ruth had asked Moth to tea, she left them alone together.

Daniel had sorted out some pieces that he

65

thought might be suitable, and he suggested playing them through without telling Moth what they were.

Moth wished she felt more at ease with him. She knew that even Ruth found him difficult to talk to, and yet after the recital he had been so friendly and helpful. I must concentrate on the music, she told herself, and shut her eyes in an effort to shut out Daniel. She didn't think he would notice.

'It's not easy to judge whether music is right for dancing to,' Miss Pearson had told her, 'but try to find something with a strong beat. And go for something you like straight away. The audience may be hearing it for the first time, and they'll be more responsive to a tune that's easy to like.'

Moth knew at once when Daniel played the right piece, but she let him finish his selection just to make sure.

'The last but one.' Daniel played a few bars. 'Yes, that's right.' Moth jumped up and began to invent some steps for it. 'Who's it by?'

'Good old Chopin. Not very original, I'm afraid, but perfect for dancing to. I thought you'd choose that one. It goes well with the Alkan, and I can play around with it a bit. Arranged by Daniel Fisher. Sounds impressive, doesn't it?'

'You must know such a lot about music. What

makes you choose to learn a piece?'

'It's not really my choice. I usually learn pieces because my teacher suggests them, and he's guided by the sort of things that are suitable for competitions. All the big international competitions have set pieces, and you need to prepare them well in advance.'

'Have you won any competitions?'

'Not yet. My first real test comes next year. Most of the competitors will be much older than me, and I'm not very likely to win. The important thing is to be heard and noticed.' Daniel was flattered by Moth's interest. 'The judges of big competitions are usually well-known musicians. Winning isn't always important. A few years ago a guy got slung out of the Chopin competition, and one of the judges thought so highly of his playing that she walked out in protest. He's famous now.'

'What's his name?'

'Ivo Pogorelich. Sounds better than Daniel Fisher, doesn't it?'

'Daniel Fisher's easier to say.'

Dan laughed. 'What's in a name? But Pogorelich is a genius, and I don't know that I'm that good.'

'You were terrific the other night. You really made me listen, and I'd only heard one of the pieces before.'

'Do you go to concerts?'

'Not often. It's so expensive, and I don't have anyone to go with. I'd rather see a ballet if I had the choice.'

'What's this?' Daniel crashed down on to the keyboard with explosive force. 'Or this?'

'Tchaikovsky, isn't it?' Moth said apprehensively. She wished she knew more about music.

'Right. The first chords were the opening of Grieg's Piano Concerto. I thought everyone knew that.'

Moth felt this was unfair. 'You do,' she said indignantly, 'because you've always lived with music, but most people have to find out for themselves, and it takes time.'

It's all very well for Daniel, with his musical parents and his grand piano, she thought, as a silence fell between them. She was glad when Ruth came in and said: 'Have you finished yet? Mummy's getting tea.'

Daniel began to play the waltz they'd chosen, and Moth started to dance to it. Ruth joined in, and the tempo got faster and faster as they whirled round the room, finally collapsing when Ruth bumped into the settee and fell headlong among the cushions.

'Mad,' said Daniel ending with a flourish, 'two mad women for the price of one.'

\* \* \*

Paul's face didn't show any feelings when Moth told him about the ballet, so she couldn't tell whether he thought it was a good or a stupid idea. He didn't say anything either when she played through the tape Daniel had made. He learned painstakingly the steps she had worked out but, as she had foreseen, he didn't dance them like a boy in love.

Moth wondered if Paul had ever been in love. His inscrutable expression made it impossible to guess what made him tick.

Libby, on the other hand, was far too responsive. She had her own ideas about the part and kept darting away from Moth saying: 'No, I feel it ought to be like this. Now if Paul goes over there . . .'

'But that's not what I've worked out,' Moth objected, feeling she was losing control. Libby threatened to snatch away the delicious new sensation of being in charge and having her own way.

When Moth had listened to the tape in her bedroom, the music had seemed as inviting as a blank sheet of paper. She had filled it with steps that formed themselves into phrases and then into sentences, and she saw that the steps were dictated by the music and by what she wanted to say. It gave her an insight into how ballets were put together, and the discovery was exciting. In her mind she invented steps for the Blue

Boy, who read her thoughts and fuelled her anguish when the other girl took him away.

Paul, however, could never be the Blue Boy, and Moth's inability to inspire him irritated and depressed her. 'It's going to be a flop,' she thought, 'and there's nothing I can do about it.'

She complained to Ruth, but Ruth was having troubles of her own with the second witch. 'She will keep saying her mother likes her to play pretty parts, and she says the words as though she was auditioning for *The Sound of Music*.'

Great-Aunt Marion was no comfort either. 'I expect the poor boy's doing his best,' she said. 'Try and see it from his point of view. Perhaps he doesn't like taking orders from you. You do sound rather bossy.'

'But it's my idea,' Moth explained for the umpteenth time. 'And he's too dull to mind about anything. He's like lumpy porridge – pale, thick, and stodgy. I hate him.'

'Well you won't get anywhere if you feel like that. Aren't you aiming a little too high? It will probably be all right on the night, and no one will notice all these finer points.'

'But *I* shall notice,' said Moth, infuriated by Gam's sweet reasonableness. 'It could be really good with the right people, and it does matter. It's the *only* thing that matters.' She took herself off to her bedroom, taking care to slam the door in protest. She knew it would annoy her great-aunt, but it served her right.

But there was one thing even worse than Paul – and that was no Paul. A few days before the show, Paul developed a bad cold, and as his mother didn't want him in bed for Christmas, she decided to keep him at home.

'Can't I have someone else?' Moth pleaded with Miss Pearson. She was prepared to make do with Drew, Nigel, anyone, but by now everyone was in something else.

'It's a shame,' Miss Pearson agreed, 'but luckily you're in the choir and the finale, and there are lots of things you can lend a hand with. Don't be too down-hearted. We can do your ballet next time.'

But Moth knew there wouldn't be a next time. By next term, the idea would have gone cold. The ballet belonged to this very important moment of her life. She had hoped to impress her parents, who were going to discuss her future with Miss Lambert, and there was Daniel too. He would be coming to see Ruth, but she wanted him to notice her and see that she did care about music, even though she hadn't recognised some silly piano concerto. Perhaps Gam was right. It's a judgement on me for criticising Paul,' she thought miserably. Oh, why does everything have to go wrong? How can I make a success of life if it all depends on someone like Paul?

The phone rang, far away, and then Gam called up the stairs: 'Moth, it's for you.'

The voice at the other end seemed to be speaking through layers of flannel, and the name Paul didn't register at first. 'Paul? Oh, Paul.' What did he want?

'I'm sorry I've been away, but I'll be back on Thursday. My mother won't let me come back any earlier, but I know the dance and we could run through it a couple of times, if you like.' Moth had never heard Paul say so much.

'That's marvellous. I'm so glad you're better. You must come back. We can't do the ballet without you.' Paul was suddenly the most desirable dancer in the world.

'Don't worry, I'll be there,' said Paul hoarsely. 'See you,' and he rang off before Moth had a chance to say any more.

Moth had been a holly berry in her first Christmas show, and she was reminded of this when she came across some of the first years rehearsing what looked like much the same ballet. They scurried out of the way when she said she wanted to use the studio, but one or two bolder ones asked if they could stay and watch. They tucked themselves into a corner and looked suitably impressed when Libby and Paul came in and began to warm up.

The stage of the school theatre was tiny compared to the stages on which Moth had danced with proper companies, but the thrill of having an audience was always the same. Moth realised with a pang that this would be her last Christmas show.

The evening always began with a commotion. Cars competed for parking space in the road outside; there were echoing voices, whispers, giggles, footsteps, lights on all over the building; figures in costume flitted across the playground to the studio, where Miss Pearson was trying desperately to get everyone to their seats in the right order, so they could file out when it was their turn to perform with the minimum disturbance.

Moth sat with the choir, but she was hardly aware of singing. She watched Libby do her other solo, with Tom, and she wasn't jealous of the applause because she knew her moment was to come.

Adrian, who was in charge of lighting, brought the lights up slowly, gradually outlining the shadowy figure against a soft blue-grey backcloth. Moth wore a full skirt and a plain white shirt draped with a black shawl that belonged to Great-Aunt Marion. It was as light

73

as thistledown, but its sombre colour gave a hint of sadness.

The audience was in a cheerful, festive mood and unprepared for the sad little tune. The sudden change of mood disconcerted them, but Moth sensed that she had caught their attention. She had to create the right impression in a couple of minutes, and she put everything else out of her mind and took hold of the wistful music as though it were a lifeline.

Then she threw off the shawl, the backcloth turned a brilliant joyous blue, and Paul sprang out of the wings. He wore a red shirt and fawn slacks, and a touch of make-up gave his face an unwonted animation. The waltz made Moth flirtatious, and she used Paul's gauche response to advantage. She was lighter and quicker than he, drawing him into a relationship that was soon threatened by the arrival of Libby. He became a prize to be competed for, with Libby's strong extrovert personality opposing Moth's slighter, more delicate movements. Libby won – as perhaps she always would – leaving a broken-hearted Moth to repeat the sad little dance of the mad woman as the backcloth faded to pale blue and then grey.

It was over – and it had come out right, thanks, Moth had to admit, to Libby and Paul. She had thought of it as her triumph, but she saw that the honours had to be shared.

Her parents thought it was 'lovely, darling', though her father said he wasn't quite sure that he'd understood it and he wished it had been a little more cheerful. Toby was more interested in the lighting effects, while Lyn, not to be outdone, announced that she, too, was going to be a dancer.

Dr Fisher congratulated Moth and asked her where she had got the idea that a man was the tool of women, and easily led by whoever took his fancy. At which Daniel laughed and said: 'Really, Dad, I don't think Moth meant anything of the kind.'

Moth wasn't quite sure what Dr Fisher meant, but it was flattering to have created something that gave people ideas – even if they were rather strange ones.

She overheard Paul's mother telling her great-aunt how thrilled Paul had been by his part, and how he had insisted on taking part, even though he wasn't fully recovered. Moth turned away, unwilling to meet Gam's eye. Paul thrilled!

But Moth didn't overhear one of the most important conversations that night. It was between Lois Taylor and one of her former pupils, who had recently become a teacher at the Fortune School. Lois was at a school of contemporary dance and taught choreography, which she said was as impossible to teach as writing or painting, because choreographers were born and could only be helped, not made.

'Any chance that girl would be interested in coming to us?' she asked, referring to Moth.

'Who? Moth Graham? I think she's keen to get into the RB if they'll have her.'

'What a pity the most promising ones always see that as the pathway to success.' Lois was an American and did not share the national pride in the Royal Ballet. 'It's all right for the tough ones and those who conform to their style, but the most exciting developments these days are happening elsewhere. That girl's got the kind of talent we're looking for, and I'm sorry it's not aimed our way.'

Nevertheless, she made a note of Moth's name.

# 9

## *A Snow Fall*

The first day of the New Year was unpromisingly grey. As one of her New Year resolutions, Moth had decided to keep a diary. It was going to be, she sensed, one of the most important years of her life, and she wanted a record to look back on.

The diary itself was a Christmas present. In asking for it, Moth had explained that she wanted something special, and her great-aunt had found it: the thick blue leather cover had Moth's initials in gold letters and the edges of the pages were tipped with gold. Best of all was the small clasp that fastened with a key, so that Moth would be able to lock her thoughts safely away.

Faced with the first page of January, she felt a certain apprehension as she looked ahead. One of the days would bring her preliminary audition for the Royal Ballet school and, if she got through, in early April there would be the final audition that would decide her future. Would she be writing down on one of these blank pages that she was among those who'd been asked to stay for the final stage?

She knew that the candidates had to do a simple class and then the names of the ones who would be examined further were called out. She remembered a girl at the Fortune telling them how awful it was, waiting to hear your name. Hers hadn't been called out, but she had soon got over the disappointment and decided to train as a teacher.

There wasn't much to write about on the first day or for the rest of the holidays, though Moth did try.

2 Jan. Went to tea with Jenny.

4 Jan. We all went to see the ballet film *The Tales of Beatrix Potter*. Toby was very bored, though he liked Jeremy Fisher.

7 Jan. Mummy bought me a new pair of shoes. Saw *The Railway Children* on TV. Quite good, but I liked the book better.

9 Jan. It snowed, and we looked at a crystal through Toby's microscope. It had beautiful patterns. Libby and Toby went tobogganing. I fell off.

Then it was back to London for the beginning

of term. There was no snow left, apart from an occasional grimy rim along the kerb and traces in the coldest corner of the garden. Great-Aunt Marion said it was too cold for more snow.

Moth and Libby were too busy to care about the weather. Their first audition was at the end of January, and their GCSEs in June began to seem uncomfortably near. Several of the others were auditioning too: Jane was now too tall, but her parents insisted on her trying; Paul had a good chance, because there was always a short-age of boys; Tom's only drawback was that he was still very short – he was sick of being called another Wayne Sleep; Linden was a quiet, deter-mined girl who had only been at the Fortune a short time.

The day before the audition the sky was a soft fleecy grey. 'It looks like snow,' Great-Aunt Marion said at breakfast, even before she heard the forecast, and she was right. It began falling at midday, and by the time Libby and Moth came home, the streets were transformed.

An arctic wind had banked up the snow, blotting out kerbs and gutters so that you couldn't see where the pavement ended. The fall was too heavy to be dissolved by the traffic, and the roads were a series of treacherous tyre tracks separated by peaks of solid discoloured icing.

The snow lodged on every ledge and crevice, delighting Moth with its inventiveness. She loved the way it outlined branches and bushes and picked out every bar of garden gates.

'If only it would last,' she said to Libby as they crunched along, turning aside every now and then to plant their footsteps on some untouched expanse. It was childish, but it was only children who really enjoyed snow.

Miss Pearson drove them to the audition, and it was all over far too soon. 'Well, that's that,' said Libby philosophically. They'd been told what to expect, but the simplicity of the tests, which included having to lie in the frog position to show the extent of their turnout, was unnerving.

Moth would have preferred being asked to perform a difficult dance, something at which it was possible to shine, instead of this quite basic assessment. One of the examiners had looked at her feet and asked if she had any trouble with *pointe* work. She had in fact been finding it painful lately, and she knew she'd blushed when she said no.

'They know what they're looking for,' said Linden, 'and we shall soon find out whether we've got it.'

'I've great hopes of all of you,' said Miss

Pearson cheerfully, 'and it isn't the end of the world if you don't get through.' But no one agreed with her.

She dropped Moth and Libby at the top of their road. No more snow had fallen, but the intense cold had prevented a thaw and the snow had become a padded quilt that squeaked as they walked on it. It was stained by shadows and dyed orange in places by the street lights. Moth shivered.

She wasn't in the mood for footprints in the snow. She wanted to get home as quickly as possible, get warm, and have supper. She hoped her great-aunt would have made one of her steak and kidney pies that gushed rich gravy when she lifted the egg-cup in the middle supporting the pastry. She savoured the contrast between the warmth and shelter just ahead and the freezing air that grazed her cheek and numbed her fingers.

She looked up in expectation as they neared the house, but the windows at the top were dark. Their morning footprints were still visible on the path, and across the lawn ran the delicate paw-marks of the downstairs cat. The urn at the foot of the steps looked like white marble, and Libby couldn't resist running her fingers round the rim and spoiling the illusion.

Moth pushed the bell and waited for her great-aunt's voice on the entry phone. 'She must be asleep,' she said to Libby, fumbling with awkward gloved fingers for the key.

But the flat was empty. They dumped their wet things in the hall and went round looking for clues. Their great-aunt had washed up the breakfast things and the kitchen had a neat folded-up air. There was no sign of a note.

'I'm starving,' said Libby. 'Let's see what there is to eat.' She began rummaging in the larder. 'Bread and butter or toast?' she asked through a mouthful of biscuit.

'I think her coat's missing,' said Moth, who didn't feel hungry any more. She had no idea of her great-aunt's plans for the day, or where to start looking for her.

'Perhaps she remembered something she wanted from the shops,' suggested Libby, stuffing some bread into the toaster. 'Do you want tea or cocoa?'

'She wouldn't go shopping now,' said Moth. 'Most of the shops would be closed. I think something's happened to her and nobody knows about us.'

Libby was buttering the toast and had decided on cocoa. 'Let's have tea first, and then if she's still not back, we'll ring up someone and ask what we should do.'

Half an hour later, Libby agreed that something must have happened to Gam. They were trying to decide who to phone – Libby thought the police was too drastic a measure – when the phone rang. It was Moth's mother.

'Where on earth have you been?' she said. 'I've been trying to ring you since four o'clock. Poor Marion has had an accident and is in hospital. Apparently she slipped in the snow and has probably broken her hip. I'm waiting to hear from the hospital.'

Moth was shocked. 'Can we go and see her?'

'Not tonight. Can you two get some supper and get yourselves off to school in the morning? I'll be down tomorrow.'

'Yes, of course. Don't worry about us, Mum . . . Gam will be all right, won't she?'

'I hope so. Broken hips are quite common at her age, but they do take a long time to mend. There's the shock too, but she's a great fighter. Now when you're cooking, be very careful to see that all the rings are switched off.'

'Oh, Mum! Don't fuss. Libby and I aren't children. See you tomorrow.'

Moth and Libby spent a subdued evening. They had the freedom that Libby at least had so wanted, but it wasn't much fun. Supper was a mixture of tins: spaghetti rings, baked beans, cocktail sausages, and some peaches in syrup. Moth felt slightly sick. They couldn't be bothered to carry the food into the living room but ate on the kitchen table to a background of pop music.

'We'll wash up in the morning,' suggested Libby, 'after breakfast. It'll take less time if we put everything together and have a grand wash.'

But later, after Libby had gone up to her room and was a cheerful noise in the distance, Moth did the washing up. She felt it was what her great-aunt would have wanted, and it made her feel better to be able to do something for her.

As she stood at the sink, she realised how much she loved Gam. She had shared with her, more than with her mother, the day-to-day problems of becoming a dancer. She didn't always take her great-aunt's advice, but she respected her old-fashioned standards, even if she wasn't sure whether they really applied to life today.

She valued, too, her great-aunt's memories of the past. Her mother couldn't tell her what her father had been like as a small boy, but Gam remembered the incidents and sayings that kept the family alive. Moth wished she'd paid more attention and asked more questions, because she saw now how fragile memories were. Libby wasn't interested in the past. For her life began anew every day. But hearing about her family and all the relatives she'd never known gave

Moth a comforting sense of belonging. There was still so much she wanted to ask her great-aunt.

Every night before she fell asleep, Moth had been saying, 'Please God let me get through this audition,' though she knew you weren't supposed to ask for things like that. But it was surely all right to say, 'Dear God, please don't let Gam die.'

# 10

## *Coping*

Great-Aunt Marion didn't die, but there was no question of her coming home soon. Mrs Graham brought with her the latest news from the hospital.

'Your great-aunt has a fractured hip. Her doctor told me it's the third case this week. He blames the weather. The pavements have been so slippery, and old people have such fragile bones. Apparently they'll have to join the bone together with a metal pin, and she'll be in hospital for at least three weeks. When she is allowed home, she'll have to take life very easy. so the next problem is how are you two going to manage?'

'We can look after ourselves,' Libby said at once. 'We can take it in turn to get meals. It'll be fun.'

Moth saw that her mother wasn't convinced.

'Fun for a day or two, perhaps, but the novelty will soon wear off when you get tired of eating out of tins and the washing-up piles up. And I don't think your great-aunt will enjoy the idea of you two at large in her flat. I'll speak to Miss Lambert and suggest you come back with me for the time being, at least until Marion is well enough to come home.'

'Oh, no!' Moth and Libby spoke as one. 'We can't miss school now. We've got GCSE, Cecchetti exams and the next audition.'

'We can't possibly be away now, Mummy,' Moth wailed. 'It would ruin everything. We're not children any more. Why can't you trust us? The worst that can happen to the flat is that it will get dirty, and you can always help us give it a spring-clean before Gam comes home. We shall only be on our own for about three weeks.'

Mrs Graham wavered. 'What about the weekends?' she said. 'I don't like the idea of your being here by yourselves. Quite apart from the question of meals, you're not old enough to be in complete charge of your lives. I know you mean well, but you don't see the dangers until it's too late.'

'Suppose we promise faithfully not to go out again after we get home from school,' said Libby persuasively. 'And you can ring us up every night to make sure we're here. If anything happened to us, the school would soon notice when we didn't turn up. Not that anything *will* happen,' she added hastily.

'Please, Mummy. We absolutely promise to come straight back here every night. We can do the shopping on Saturday. It'll be fun finding different things to eat. We don't bother much now because Gam likes shopping and cooking, but we ought to learn how to look after ourselves, and then we'll be able to help look after Gam when she comes home.'

'Well, if you're sure you don't mind being on your own. But I shall have a word with Miss Lambert and make sure she knows what the situation is. And if there are any problems, or anything goes wrong, back you come.'

Miss Lambert agreed that Moth and Libby were old enough to look after themselves. 'Don't worry, we'll keep an eye on them,' she assured Mrs Graham, 'and I'm sure their friends will lend a hand. Moth's very friendly with Ruth Fisher, and I know Mrs Fisher won't mind an extra mouth or two. She's very generous and hospitable.'

Another surprising ally was Tom's mother, Mrs Blundell-Smith. As always, she relished a crisis and was very willing to come to the aid of any victims.

'I'm afraid the old lady will be out of action

for weeks,' she told Mrs Graham. 'The same thing happened to an aunt of mine, and it was months before she could walk again. The doctors are far too optimistic. But don't worry about the girls. They'll be company for Tom, and when you've got to shop and cook for three, what difference do another two make?'

Quite a lot, thought Mrs Graham, remembering how much Libby ate, but she didn't want to discourage Mrs Blundell-Smith, who could certainly afford a couple of extra mouths.

'So it's all settled,' she explained to Moth and Libby when they arrived home from school. 'Miss Lambert, Mrs Fisher and Mrs Blundell-Smith are going to keep an eye on you, and they'll help with any problems. I've been shopping and stocked up the larder and the fridge. You'll have to cope with things like milk and bread and eggs, but you've got plenty of cornflakes, tins of soup, baked beans, hamburgers, fishfingers, some of those frozen pizzas you like, and . . .'

'Fine,' said Moth, wishing her mother wasn't quite so efficient. She'd looked forward to going shopping and choosing for herself. How bossy parents were! They always assumed they were the only ones who knew how to do things.

'Now don't forget to check that the oven's switched off. I know I sound fussy, but it's easily done. And don't have the immersion on all the time. And make sure all the lights are turned off and the front door's locked, and don't answer the door to any strange men.'

'Mummy! Stop it. You'll miss your train if you don't go. Just trust us and everything will be all right.'

Mrs Graham had only been gone a few minutes before the bell rang.

'Don't answer,' warned Libby. 'It might be a tall dark stranger.' But Moth guessed who it was. A voice still charged with anxiety came over the entry phone.

'Don't forget to visit your great-aunt. I said you'd go at the weekend. Perhaps you could take her something to read.'

They waited expectantly for still more reminders, but this time Mrs Graham had finally gone.

The flat seemed very still, as though no one lived there any more. Moth wandered round to see if anything needed doing, but her mother had dusted, polished and plumped up the cushions and everywhere was just as Great-Aunt Marion liked it.

Libby felt the stillness too, and did something about it. She fetched her CD player, put on a disc, and for the first time in its history Great-Aunt Marion's quiet drawing room began to rock.

# 11

## *Moth's Night Out*

'You've got the guest room,' said Ruth, taking Moth to a part of the house that she hadn't seen before. 'A sculptor used to live here, and Daddy says he built this room as a studio. He must have made enormous statues, because it's got such a high ceiling, and it was no use to us until Daddy had the brainwave of converting it into a garage with a bedroom on top.'

A wooden staircase linked the room to the rest of the house. The huge skylight designed by the sculptor was still there, but it was curtained by a striped blind.

When Ruth left Moth to unpack her things – she hadn't brought much as she was only staying for the weekend – Moth tried out the bed and found herself looking up into a roof of green and white stripes that reminded her of a circus tent. Or perhaps it's like being in a balloon, she thought, feeling as though the room had cut loose and was drifting away.

The Fishers, it seemed, never threw anything away, and the guest room was a kind of glory-hole to which all sorts of odds and ends had been banished. Moth had never seen walls so crowded with pictures. Someone had collected engraved views of abbeys and cathedrals in black and gold frames, but she preferred the little watercolour of a street-market scene in which one of the stalls had a striped awning like the one above her.

The picture she liked best was of a cat fast asleep on a velvet button-back chair like one her great-aunt had. Outside the window, at work cleaning it, was a man on a ladder, and Moth enjoyed the contrast between the contented cat, warm inside, and the man outside on what she felt was a chill winter afternoon.

Catching sight of her hair in a mirror, she began searching for a comb in her holdall. On the chest of drawers beside the mirror was a group of tiny vases and jugs decorated with the arms of seaside towns, and some photographs of Daniel and Ruth that had been taken years ago. One of them showed baby Daniel hauling himself to his feet by grasping at the leg of a piano. Moth guessed he would be annoyed if he knew she'd seen it. Toby got furious if her mother dared to leave around any pictures of him when he was little.

Some of the photographs were of a much older generation, and one of them was inside a pretty carved case. Moth was disconcerted to see her own face looking out from the scrolled mount, but then she tilted the frame and saw that the mirror glass contained the image of a couple. The woman, wearing a tight-waisted taffeta dress, had her arm in that of a serious young man who was forced to keep his chin up by a tall stiff collar. She wondered whether they might be Daniel's great-grandparents, and was trying to decide whether there was any family resemblance when she heard Ruth calling, 'Moth, are you ready? It's time for lunch.'

Perhaps it's rude to look at other people's belongings, Moth thought, hastily snapping the lid back on the couple. She wouldn't have admitted it to Ruth, but one of the reasons she'd so looked forward to staying with her was that she found her home so intriguing and had always wanted the chance to explore it.

Lunch was an ordeal. Moth's family sat round the kitchen table, but the Fishers ate in the dining room at a polished, formally laid table, with the food brought in on a trolley.

The food, too, was different – everything seemed to be smoked or pickled and was very spicy – and Moth didn't like to object when Mrs Fisher loaded her plate as though she hadn't eaten for a fortnight.

She sat opposite Dr Fisher, who meant well but made her feel as though she was taking an exam – and failing.

'I see you're admiring my Friedrich,' he said, to Moth's embarrassment. What had she done, and what on earth was he talking about? Unexpectedly, Daniel came to her rescue.

'My father expects everyone to share his taste, but I think it's a very gloomy picture.'

Moth realised that she'd been looking in the direction of a strange moonlit landscape. She wasn't sure whether to agree with Daniel and perhaps offend Dr Fisher, so she said: 'I've been looking at the pictures in my room. I like the one with the cat.'

Dr Fisher smiled. 'If you like pictures, I must give you a conducted tour. The Friedrich belonged to my father. He believed that pictures should be enjoyed at home, where you can see them in different lights and different moods, not stuck in galleries where no one really looks at them.'

Moth looked down at her plate. She didn't know what to say, and it seemed safer to concentrate on eating.

'How about a second helping?' Mrs Fisher

looked so pleased by her appetite that Moth felt she couldn't say no, though she didn't really like the pickled fish.

'Just a little, then.'

It was Dr Fisher's turn to be helpful. 'Have you any plans for the rest of the day?'

'Well, I'm going to the Albert Hall this evening,' Daniel announced. 'Bishop-Kovacevich is playing the Beethoven Four and I want to see what he makes of it.'

'It would be more polite to ask our guest what she would like to do, instead of telling us you're off.'

Daniel scowled. 'I'm sorry. She can come if she likes. So can Ruth. It's a very pop programme, just right for beginners.'

He's being superior again, thought Moth, just like he used to be. It wasn't a very gracious invitation, and what was she supposed to say? She tried to catch Ruth's eye, but Ruth was fiddling with her spoon.

'Do you want to go out on a cold night?' asked Mrs Fisher, trying to sweeten everyone with the offer of cheesecake or apple strudel. 'Wouldn't it be nicer to stay in front of the fire? We could listen to some music or Dan could play for us.'

Daniel groaned. 'What on earth does the weather matter? We're not a pack of old ladies likely to catch cold. Recorded music isn't the same as the real thing. I'm going, and Ruth and "our guest" can do what they like.'

'Well if you do decide to go,' said Dr Fisher, 'make up your minds this afternoon. Don't all rush off at the last minute just as we're about to have supper.'

Moth was relieved when the meal was over. She and Ruth cleared away while Daniel took himself off to practise.

'Does he play every day?' she asked, as they stacked the plates in the dishwasher. She would like to have listened to Daniel playing, even scales.

'Usually. He's going in for a scholarship to go somewhere like Paris or Moscow. He doesn't think about anything else.'

Moth was silent. Ruth might be her best friend, but she was the one person she could never tell about her liking for Daniel – when he was in a good mood. Ruth wouldn't understand, especially when she had to cope with a situation in which although she was younger, he was the adored, indulged one of the family.

'You want to go to the concert, don't you?' Ruth made it sound more like an accusation than a question.

Moth turned away to get some more plates from the trolley. She felt as though Ruth had been reading her thoughts. 'I've never been to the Albert Hall,' she said defensively, 'but you choose. What would you like to do?'

'Go and see a really scary film,' said Ruth unexpectedly. 'One with forces of evil and things coming out of graves. But Daddy wouldn't pay for that. You don't know how lucky you are, not having parents around to take a close interest in you and try to make you cultured.'

'But . . .' Moth had often envied Ruth her background: the house full of music, parents who talked about books and art and went to see plays, operas and ballets. Now she wasn't so sure. Perhaps it was better to discover things for yourself and not feel under an obligation to like them. 'I'll come to a film with you,' she promised, 'if you'll come to the concert tonight.'

'OK. But it's a pity we have to go with Dan. We can't have a proper talk when he's around.'

She hasn't guessed, Moth thought with relief, as they went off to tell Mrs Fisher.

Daniel had been told to pay for everything and he enjoyed being in charge. He bought seats on the side where they could watch the pianist's hands, and wasn't superior when Moth admitted that she hadn't been to the Albert Hall before.

She shared his fondness for the crimson grandeur of the auditorium – like a giant opera-house – with its tiers of boxes, each with neat red curtains parted at an angle that reminded her of the way she had drawn windows as a child.

Once, as a small boy, Daniel told her, when he'd come with his mother, who belonged to a choral society, he'd run all round the hall while she was rehearsing, and then been allowed to stand on the conductor's rostrum.

'I nearly changed my mind about wanting to be a pianist. I remember looking up at the boxes and imagining myself conducting the audience as well as the orchestra. The sense of power was intoxicating.'

Moth looked up at the dome and felt dizzy. There were people standing right at the top, and she felt nervous at the mere thought of the drop. She pointed them out to Ruth, who said: 'I've been up there for the Proms. I like it, but Dan's scared of heights and insists on going in the middle.'

Something I've got in common with Dan, Moth thought, secretly pleased.

The first item on the programme, an overture, was over before Moth could decide whether to watch the orchestra or shut her eyes and listen. She didn't seem able to do both at once. She wondered whether it would help to know something about the music, and she read her programme as, to ironic cheers, the piano was wheeled on. She tried to concentrate on the words, but it didn't mean much to learn, for example, that the rondo began with pianissimo strings suggesting the key of C, which Beethoven, with characteristic humour, steered adroitly back to G.

But as soon as the piano stuttered the opening quavers, quickly repeated and expanded by the orchestra, she knew that it didn't matter. The runs up and down the keyboard, the sparkling trills, the satisfying way in which the notes sped up and down ladders of sound, made a pattern that paralleled her shifting feelings, so that whenever she heard it afterwards, Moth could recall the uncertain excitement of Dan there beside her, absorbed in his score.

They gave up the idea of an interval coffee when they saw the length of the queues, and set off instead to walk right round the hall. The echoing corridor reminded Moth of an anti-quated school where she had once had dancing lessons; it, too, had been painted a dingy buff.

Daniel and Ruth vied with memories of other concerts, and when Moth was beginning to be envious of their talk of the Proms, Daniel said: 'You must come this year. Being thrown in at the deep end is the best way of learning about music. Dad gave me a season ticket last year, and I went nearly every night. By the end, there was music in my head all the time. I felt as though it was going on inside me, like blood in my veins.'

If only Daniel meant it about the Proms! Moth had found that when most people said you must come next time, come to tea, or to stay with us when we're up in Scotland, or down in Cornwall, or some other place you'd always longed to go, they were only being polite and didn't mean it. But even if Daniel forgot, Moth knew that she would be coming to the Albert Hall again, that it had a part in the future.

'It's an old warhorse,' Daniel said of the symphony that filled the second half of the concert. But Moth, who feared a symphony might be long and boring, found it tuneful and stirring, with thunder and lightning on the drums. The oboe sang a wistful little tune that Dvorak had picked up from the slaves when he visited the New World, and it seemed so familiar that Moth couldn't tell whether she had heard it before or whether, as Daniel had described, the music had got into her veins.

She felt a sense of loss when it was over, and went on clapping to put off going home, but the orchestra – thirsty men all – were quick to dismantle their instruments and Ruth, impatient, said there were dumplings for supper.

Outside it was raining. Moth and Ruth pulled up the hoods of their anoraks, but Daniel had no protection and the rain flattened his hair into the dark glistening skin of a seal.

'Run for it,' he said, and they linked arms and splashed across the ribbons of light that wavered on the pavement. The rain came at them, hemming their faces with watery stitches, and Moth could feel her programme buckling in the front of her anorak, where she had tucked it to keep it dry.

The journey back was a series of frustrating waits, with time to read all the posters including the one that offered a prize if it contained your address. 'Though it never does!' Ruth complained, after they had located an unlikely Mr Smith of 10 The Avenue. A group of youths were assaulting a slot machine, tugging at the drawers and then kicking the sides as the machine refused to give in. The other passengers huddled in the middle of the platform – it might be their turn next.

Then they were back in the rain, running past shoals of parked cars, down a street where most of the houses had been divided up into flats. Lights were on in the basements, and Moth saw fleetingly into rooms decorated with posters and Indian bedspreads; then round the corner into the Fishers' street, where the houses were shielded by front gardens patrolled by well-bred cats.

The rain skidded to a halt as Mrs Fisher

opened the door, and confronted it with a spicy warmth. But the first words after her greeting were not so comforting.

As Moth and Ruth shed their sodden coats and Daniel went off to towel his hair, she said, almost apologetically: 'Moth, my dear, do you know anything about Libby's plans? Mrs Blundell-Smith has just rung up in a great state. Apparently Libby and Tom have gone to a party, and she doesn't know where. She seemed to think you would know.'

But Moth didn't. She had no idea where Libby might have gone, but her old resentment of her cousin welled up. She won't come to any harm, she thought bitterly, she never does, but she always manages to involve me in some way – just when we promised that nothing would go wrong.

# 12

## Libby's Night Out

The address Evan had given Libby was only a short drive from the Blundell-Smiths'. It was a respectable-looking street of large old houses, built at a time when most families could afford live-in servants. Now even the cook's basement and the maid's attic had been turned into flats.

Libby and Tom tried to work out the street numbers.

'I think it's this one, Dad,' said Tom.

Mr Blundell-Smith pulled up and they tumbled from the cosseting warmth of the car's back seat into the watery stain of a streetlight. Mr Blundell-Smith, anxious not to miss the start of a snooker championship on television, drove swiftly off, leaving Libby and Tom in front of a flight of steps that led up to an imposing entrance.

'Is this the right place?' said Tom doubtfully.

'Evan said 69.' The bells offered a bewildering choice of occupants. 'I don't remember his friend's name, so we'll have to take a chance.'

Libby pressed a bell and tried to see through the door. Panes of coloured glass dyed the inside ruby red and royal blue.

'Try another one,' said Tom, and pressed a selection of bells for good measure.

'Idiot! You'll have everyone coming, and they won't be pleased.'

They waited apprehensively, ready to run. Finally the door was opened a fraction by an elderly lady who was plainly not giving a party.

'What do you want?' She sounded scared rather than cross.

Libby stood her ground, but Tom was already two steps down. 'I'm sorry we disturbed you, but we've come to a party. We must have rung the wrong bell.'

Another occupant, this time a young man who'd run all the way downstairs – perhaps in hopes of a girlfriend – had appeared. 'I guess you want 69b,' he said, catching his breath. 'It's the basement. Go down the steps at the side.'

'Thanks.' Tom knocked into a row of dustbins and a lid clattered down into the area. The side of the house was ominously dark, and they had to feel their way along. They found the door almost by accident, and after rattling and bang-ing on it, stood well clear; Tom crossed his fingers and hoped there weren't any dogs. They could hardly see the figure who answered their summons, but Libby didn't think it was Evan.

'We're friends of Evan,' she said boldly. 'He asked us to a party.'

The figure moved back and, when they hesitated, said gruffly: 'Well don't just stand there. Come on in.'

Tom would have liked to turn back, even if it meant walking home and thinking up some story for his mother, but he dared not leave Libby. He followed her in, threw his jacket after hers, and went towards a flicker of light.

But for the floor, which was bright green, the long room might have been hewn out of coal, for the walls and ceiling were a glinting glossy black. On the wall facing Tom was a full-length mirror, and for a moment he thought that some hideous force had transformed Libby and him into grotesques.

The boy who had shown them in saw his reaction and laughed.

'Good, isn't it? Hyde got it from a funfair.'

The room was lit from the floor, like the footlights of a stage, and the lamps were masked by green filters so that their light was unearthly. The party had not begun yet and a group was setting up its gear at the far end of the room.

'Albert,' called the boy, 'some friends of yours.'

The drummer looked in their direction. He didn't look too pleased to see them, and a boy with a guitar remarked: 'Is this yer fan club? Bit small, aren't they?'

Evan was no longer the boy behind the counter selling discs. He wore white jeans and a black T-shirt, and like the others in the group, he had a green streak in his hair. Green-rimmed sunglasses with mirror lenses hid his eyes and threw back distorted reflections. He looked taller, too.

'Hi!' said Libby.

'You're early,' said Evan-Albert. 'We shan't be starting a set much before ten.'

'Why did he call you Albert?'

'Part of the new image. We've reformed the band. Probably going to change the name. Hyde wants a completely new band. Says we'd never get anywhere as we were.'

'Which is Hyde?' asked Tom nervously.

'Lead singer. Calls himself Hyde Park. I'm Albert Hall, and the guy on bass is Ken Gore. He's a bit of a creep, but Hyde is terrific. He was at art school and he's got style. Wait till you hear our new sound.'

A girl wearing a black beret and dark glasses swaggered up to Tom and burst out laughing at his scared expression.

'Are you two just going to stand around all night, or could you bear to help?'

'Doing what?' Libby spoke for both of them.

'Bringing in the food. There are some packing cases in the hall. If you' – she looked at Tom – 'could bring them in here, we could put the food on top of them.'

The girl took Libby into a cupboard at the end of the hall which served as a kitchen. In the sink was a washing-up bowl full of panes of green glass.

'It's jelly,' the girl explained. 'Hyde's mad about jelly. Says it's good for you.'

Libby was glad she'd had supper first. Hyde, it seemed, was a vegetarian: a huge battered saucepan seethed with brown rice, while the rest of the stove was occupied by a cauldron that could well, Libby felt, have contained eye of newt and toe of frog, though the girl said it was pulses.

'Hyde hasn't worked out how everyone will eat it. There are some cups and bowls in the cupboard, and he's borrowing stuff from the guy upstairs. Could you take these into the other room.'

She handed Libby a pile of none-too-clean

saucers. Tom and Evan had made a counter of packing cases in one corner, and Libby stacked the saucers on it.

By now a steady stream of couples was arriving, and Libby and the girl began spooning the rice and pulses into the assortment of china. It must have tasted better than it looked, for several of the boys came back for seconds. They washed it down with a variety of drinks in cans, and Libby grabbed herself a Coke. Tom told her the green jelly wasn't bad.

'Make your hair curl,' said Hyde playfully, holding out a heavy glass ashtray for more pulses. Libby saw herself in his glasses and stared back, determined not to show that he frightened her. Close to, he wasn't much older than Evan, and his insolent looks sparked off a curious excitement, like touching a live wire. She was conscious that he was looking her over.

'Didn't know Albert went in for cradle-snatching,' he said. 'What do you do – sing or something?'

Libby scraped together the last of the pulses before she said, as casually as possible: 'I dance.'

'What kind of dancing?'

'Depends on the music.' Libby sensed that ballet was not the right image, and she wasn't giving Hyde the chance to score off her.

He looked amused. He drained his Coke and

considered her, almost mockingly. 'I'll look out for you,' he said. 'My kind of dancing's not for little girls.' And he turned away.

The room had filled up, and the acrid air made Libby's eyes water; it was a fierce mixture of smoke, sweat, and an excitement that crackled like static. Then the band began to play.

They were louder and more overpowering than on their recording. As their rhythm reached out across the room, Tom and Libby began to dance – not a dance Mrs Blundell-Smith would have recognised.

The music told them what they wanted to hear: it shouted out that they were alive, they were young, they were full of energy. It was violent. It expressed anger against a world that resented their youth. It was against restrictions, rules, lack of opportunity, being old, a world ready-made by other people. It was for being young, having ideals and ambitions, everything new, boundless energy. It took Libby and Tom away from great-aunts and mothers and joined them to their own generation; it gave them, as though on a shining platter, their inheritance. They lost all sense of time: nothing mattered but obedience to a sound that drowned out all loyalties and led them into a world of pure movement.

Libby was a fragment in a kaleidoscope of

revolving shapes and lights, and it was some moments before she realised that the shapes nearest the door were not dancing but fighting. Someone threw a can and hit one of the spots, splintering the coloured filter and exposing a harsh, naked light.

The band stopped playing and Hyde, dazzled, tried to make out what was going on. The aggression of the music had been a fantasy; what was happening by the door was for real.

Tom edged closer to Libby and she sensed his fear. She herself felt indignant rather than scared. Why, when everything was so marvellous, did this have to happen?

The fight was spreading, as people trying to get away from the area of trouble were thrust against each other and struck out to protect themselves. The newcomers were trying to wreck the music equipment. Libby heard the crunch of things breaking, glasses, crockery, wood, and dodged as someone began hurling empty cans.

'Let's go,' implored Tom, clutching her to avoid being swept away.

Libby saw Hyde, haloed with a green light, hugging his guitar and weaving from side to side like a boxer. She had no idea who was attacking who, or why. Probably word had got round that there was a party and mates, rivals, total

111

strangers, thought it fun to break it up.

As Libby and Tom edged towards the door, they found that the packing cases had been stacked up into a barricade; those sheltering behind were pelting the enemy with anything to hand. Tom was hit by a gobbet of pulses, now congealed into a messy weapon.

Just as they reached the door, a group of youths ran full tilt into the barricade and catapulted one of the crates in the direction of the window. The tinkle of broken glass brought a momentary surprised silence; then the sound of blows and breakages increased.

'Our coats!' yelled Libby, scrabbling at the mountain of discarded clothing. Tom pulled at random, spilling the pile so that coats and jackets toppled in all directions. 'Ours'll be at the bottom,' said Libby. 'We were almost the first here.' Miraculously the bottom layer had survived intact, and she dragged out their jackets triumphantly.

It was a relief to be assailed by the driving rain. They scrambled up the dank area steps and were at the gate when they heard the police siren.

'Quick! Run!' shouted Tom, and as they clattered down the street a police car swooped round the corner, its warning lights flashing agitatedly. It stopped outside the house and a

couple of uniformed men got out and disappeared down the steps.

'We might have been arrested!' Tom was appalled.

'I wonder what'll happen now?' Libby, glad to have escaped, had immediately recovered her buoyancy. 'I hope they arrest those awful gate-crashers. It was a super party until they arrived.'

Tom huddled into his jacket. He felt cold, wet, miserable, and lost. He realised that he didn't know the way home. 'Where are we?' he said, twisting his head so that the hood of his coat partly blinded him.

'No idea. I thought you knew. It's your part of London.'

'Well, I don't know it that well, silly. I don't often go for walks in the dark.'

The streets were lined with identical houses. The only landmark, a church spire, confirmed after a while that they were going round in circles.

'We ought to have hung round the house,' said Tom. 'We could have waited outside until my father came.'

Libby couldn't be bothered to point out that it was Tom who had started running when he saw the police car. She was too wet to fight back; her earlier exhilaration seemed light years away. Was it really only an hour ago that she'd been dancing to Hyde, dancing for Hyde, bound to him by his music? Now the everyday world had returned with a vengeance. She could imagine the kind of scene that would take place when the Blundell-Smiths discovered that the party had ended in a police raid.

'We can't wander round all night,' said Tom wearily. 'There'll be a row whatever we do, and I don't think I'll ever find the way back. Let's find a phone box and ask them to come and get us.'

It wasn't an area where people seemed to need phone boxes, but at last they found one, and an exhausted Tom dialled the operator and asked her to reverse the charges.

He held the phone away from his ear, as though his mother was likely to leap out of it, and Libby, too, heard her voice.

'Darling, where are you? We've been terribly worried. Have you been waiting hours for Daddy?'

'No,' said Tom, dazed. 'We tried to walk home and got lost.'

'Tell me where you are. Don't move. We'll be right over.'

The journey back was a monologue by an overwrought Mrs Blundell-Smith. It seemed that Mr Blundell-Smith, concentrating on the snooker, had forgotten the address and couldn't

115

find the right street. He'd been driving round looking for them, until he decided that they would probably realise something was wrong.

'You should have phoned from your friends,' said Mrs Blundell-Smith reprovingly, 'instead of wandering about on a night like this. There are some very rough people around. You might have been attacked by one of those awful gangs.'

In the warmth and safety of the back seat Tom nudged Libby and sneezed.

'Lemon, honey and asprin for you,' said Mrs Blundell-Smith. 'I don't want to say I told you so, but I think we might all have been better off with an evening at home. You don't want a cold with your Royal Ballet audition coming up.'

Libby was tempted to say, 'You're lucky all Tom's got are a few sneezes. He might have been beaten up.' Poor Tom! She didn't think he'd enjoyed any of the evening that much, whereas she had glimpsed the future and couldn't wait to be free to explore it.

# 13

## *Up to a Point*

'. . . and she was so busy fussing over Tom's chest that she forgot to ask about the party, so we didn't have to tell any lies after all.'

'But you'd told quite a lot in the first place,' Moth pointed out. 'Honestly, Libby, fancy saying that Gam knew all about the party and had said we could go. If I'd got back earlier and had to speak to Mrs B-S, it would all have come out, and I'd have been dragged in, and she'd be bound to have told Mummy.'

'Life is about taking risks,' said Libby, as undaunted as ever. 'You don't achieve anything by staying at home, and I'm glad I went. It was worth it just to see Hyde – '

'He sounds like some kind of tearaway. I don't know what you see in someone like that.'

'Tastes differ. Some people can see things in precious stuck-up pianists – '

'Dan's not . . .' Moth, quick to come to Daniel's defence, blushed as she realised that Libby had noticed her interest.

Libby helped herself to another biscuit – there was only one left. 'Your turn to get the fish and chips, and then I suppose we'd better do some washing-up.'

'I'm so glad Gam's coming home,' said Moth, relieved that Libby had changed the subject. 'It'll be marvellous to have real food again.'

There were limits, she'd discovered, to her appetite for things on toast, chips, crispy pancake rolls (Libby's favourite), and even pizzas.

But although Great-Aunt Marion was determined to get back on her feet, she was declared housebound for the first few weeks and had to be content with hopping around on crutches. She had become, it seemed to Moth, smaller and more frail, as though the fracture had also breached her defence against growing old; but her spirit was obstinately defiant.

'Thank you, but no,' she said firmly, when the health visitor mentioned Meals on Wheels. 'They are for the elderly and handicapped. I still have all my faculties and two energetic nieces. I'm sure we can manage.'

And manage they did, though Libby grumbled at having to do the washing-up every evening and accused her great-aunt – though not in her hearing – of being too proud to accept proper help.

They were under pressure at school too, with the threat of GCSE brandished at nearly every lesson and the approach of the all-important audition.

'Not that it'll do you any good,' said Miss Pearson briskly when Jane, who was unexpectedly in the final audition, brought a note from her parents asking for extra classes.

'You're not going to dazzle them with some sudden burst of talent you've picked up at the last minute. What they're looking for is long-term potential, qualities that will blossom under their special training and, above all, the right kind of physique. You've either got it or you haven't, and you'll be at your best if you just try and relax.'

Moth was tempted to ask Miss Pearson about her foot, which was increasingly painful after *pointe* work, but she told herself that this was normal – surely she'd read of dancers bravely going on with bleeding toes. She'd know soon enough anyway if something was seriously wrong because Marsha, who had auditioned the previous year and was now happily doing stage dancing, had told them what to expect.

'They divide you up into . . . I think it was three groups – about twenty in each – and then you do a simple class. *Pliés, fondus, battements,* the usual sort of thing. And they watch you like hawks.

'Who's "they"?'

'There were four of them; one was the principal and I suppose the others were teachers. They ask you to do frogs to show your turnout, and they push your legs to see if the hip joint is free. That's all. I kept thinking, how can my whole future depend on something so ordinary as a simple, everyday class.'

'And that's it?' In one of her favourite fantasies, Moth had often seen herself giving such an inspired display that she was offered a place on the spot.

'Well, that's all I did.' Marsha would have liked to have made more of her story, and perhaps scared that spoilt Jane. 'We were asked to wait while they compared notes, and then they called out the names of those they wanted to stay on. I wasn't one of them, so I don't know what happened next.'

'I shall cry,' said Jane, who expected to be chosen. 'I know I shall cry if they don't call out my name.'

And sure enough she did.

She was not the only one, though Moth was determined not to show her feelings. It had all been as Marsha said: a simple class taken by a brisk young teacher who gave them a brief reassuring smile before leading them into *pliés*, etc. Then they changed shoes for *pointe* work.

The studio, with its mirrors and barres, was like all the others Moth had practised in over the years, and the other students, as they were called now, only a step away from the confident, purposeful adults who had jostled past them in the entrance hall, off to rehearse with Darcey, Phillip, Bruce, Deborah – They all looked calm and serious, though inside they were probably as tense and nervous as Moth was.

'Wonder what they're saying?' said Tom, more to pass the time than because he expected an answer.

'They were writing things down,' said Libby, who had kept an eye on the auditioners. 'And they found us funny. Two of them were whispering – like we're not allowed to – and trying hard not to laugh.'

'I don't feel like laughing,' wailed Jane. 'I think I'm going to be sick.'

Tom, helpfully, pointed out the fire-bucket, and the girls had just decided to go in search of the loo, when one of the auditioners returned and they froze like statues.

The names were called alphabetically, so Tom came first.

'Tom Blundell-Smith.' He grinned with relief.

Everyone else seemed to begin with F . . .
Foster . . . Forsyth . . . Fraser . . . Those at the
end of the alphabet looked despairing.

'Elizabeth Graham.' Moth looked down. She
would be next, if chosen . . .

'Jennifer Graham.'

It was like musical chairs. She had survived
for the moment, but only a handful of the last
thirty would finally get a place.

Moth knew on the way home that she hadn't
made it. While Libby and Tom kept up their
spirits by being rude about the other hopefuls,
Moth was silent.

It was no use pretending; she knew. Knew
that she wouldn't be going to Talgarth Road,
wouldn't be learning the repertoire, covering
rehearsals, waiting for the chance – because
someone was suddenly sick or injured – that
would magically put her on stage in the back
row of the *corps de ballet*. None of that would
happen. She wouldn't ever be a little swan – and
she'd often linked hands with imaginary cygnets
to that jaunty little tune – or ever dance at
Covent Garden.

Her eyes prickled at the unfairness of it all:
she had been deceived by dreams that spurred
her into practising, by teachers who'd encour-
aged her when they ought to have known . . .
Her anger and resentment became an anguish

that made her feel sick. Noise, lights, movement stabbed at her head, yelling in triumph as they made her wince. Getting home seemed an almost impossible goal, and once there she went straight to her room and fell on the bed, burying her head beneath the welcome darkness of the pillow.

Libby told her worried great-aunt: 'Moth doesn't want any supper. She's got a bit of a headache.'

The pain was gone by the next morning, but Moth couldn't face going to school. What was the point? It was all over, everything she'd been aiming for all her life, and dancing no longer seemed important. She lay there feeling numb, drained, remembering the hours she'd spent practising, wondering how many classes she'd done over the years ... She couldn't recall a time when she hadn't danced – and apparently it had all been for nothing.

When Libby breezed in to ask how she felt, Moth burrowed under the clothes and said she still felt sick ... not well enough to go to school today ... not well enough to go ever again, she wanted to say.

'OK. I'll tell Gam. Do you want anything – orange juice, cornflakes?' Libby's tone implied that she thought Moth was shamming.

'No thanks.'

Later Moth heard the front door slam and felt relieved that Libby had gone. I shall put everything away, she thought, looking fretfully round the room. All those ridiculous reminders of being a dancer that had betrayed her, fired her enthusiasm for a way of life that was now to be denied her. They had tempted and tantalised her, only to snatch away the prize as she reached out for it.

She heard the downstairs clock strike the half-hour and then the silence resumed. It felt unnatural to be doing nothing in time that properly belonged to school. She pictured them in class, having a verb test, getting their history essays back – she was sorry to miss that, as she was secretly proud of hers – but there was nothing there that would tell her what to do with the rest of her life now that she couldn't be a dancer.

She got up, pulled on jeans and a T-shirt, and unearthed an old sweater with frayed elbows. It felt comforting and don't-carish, though it didn't do anything for the cold deep inside her.

Her great-aunt was still in bed, but she heard Moth moving around and called to her.

Moth drifted into her bedroom.

'Libby said you weren't well. Are you feeling better?'

Moth shrugged her shoulders. 'S'pose so.'

Moth, who was incandescent when she was happy, drooped like a flower out of water. She's so transparent, her great-aunt thought, so easily cast down. She was afraid of saying the wrong thing, but she sensed that Moth needed to talk.

'Tell me what happened yesterday. Did something go wrong?'

Moth's mouth trembled and she burst out: 'It's so unfair. Why let me go on dancing all this time if I haven't got the right kind of feet. Why didn't someone say so, ages ago?'

'Is that what the school said?'

'More or less. I was so pleased when I got through to the second round. I thought it was going to be all right. We had to do a few dance sequences and then we were examined by a doctor. He asked lots of questions and took lots of measurements, and then he looked at my feet and asked if I had any pain with them. My right foot does hurt sometimes, though I've tried not to admit it, and then he said something about having a high extended instep. I asked him if that was bad, and he said that it would see me through life all right, but if I became a dancer I would be asking it to take a tremendous amount of strain, especially with *pointe* work, and I could end up crippled. He tried to explain, but I didn't really take in what he was saying . . . I just knew that I wouldn't get a place . . . that it didn't matter how hard I'd worked . . .'

Moth was crying now. 'I wouldn't have minded,' she sobbed, 'if I hadn't been good enough, if I hadn't worked hard, but it isn't my fault; it was all decided in advance – in a sense when I was born – and I never knew . . .'

She sat down on the bed and her great-aunt put her arms around her. 'Moth, dear, I'm so sorry. What a terrible disappointment, and how awful for you to find out like that.' She stroked Moth's hair gently and Moth inhaled a faint scent of distant flowers. 'No wonder you felt rotten last night. I wish I'd known. I hate to think of you going off to bed early by yourself. I wanted to come and see you, but I can't manage the stairs with those wretched crutches. What a pair we are: both wounded warriors.'

'I don't know what to do,' Moth confessed. 'I've never thought of becoming anything but a dancer. There really isn't anything else I want to be. Honestly, Gam, I'm not just being difficult.'

'You feel that now, but you need time to adjust. Nobody knows what to do at first when they lose something important in their lives, but the answer will turn up, however impossible it seems now.'

'I know one thing: I'm not going back to school.'

'Well, I don't suppose it'll matter for a few

days. You may feel different next week.'

'I won't,' Moth said firmly. 'If I can't dance, then I don't want any more to do with dancing: no more classes, no more shows, nothing.'

Great-Aunt Marion didn't argue; she saw that Moth was in no mood to listen to reason, but Moth's mother was less understanding when she rang up that evening.

'Don't be silly, darling, of course you must go back to school. You must finish off the year at the Fortune, do your GCSEs, and then we can decide what to do next.'

'I want to go to another school.'

'All right, dear, but you can't change just now with the exams only two or three months away. Try and be sensible.'

'I'm not ever going to set foot in the Fortune again. I hate it. I hate all the teachers. It's their silly fault this has happened. They should have known about my feet . . .' Moth dissolved into angry tears.

'Perhaps they should' – her mother was trying to appease Moth – 'but you are rather jumping to conclusions. After all, you haven't heard definitely that you haven't got a place.'

'I haven't, I haven't . . .' Moth shouted into the receiver. 'Don't be so stupid. They've got plenty of other girls to choose from, girls like Libby who've got the right kind of feet . . .'

Libby . . . She couldn't bear to think of Libby
being offered a place.

'We're not getting anywhere like this. You're
obviously in one of your difficult moods. I'd
like a word with Marion – I hope you're not
taking it out on her.'

'No, I'm not, because she's not like you. She
knows what dancing means to me, and she can
understand why I don't want to go to school
. . .' Moth slammed the phone down and went
off to her room as her great-aunt, looking concerned, hobbled into the hall.

Moth stuck to her decision not to go to school
for the rest of the week. No one, not even
Libby, said anything about it, and her great-aunt
seemed positively to enjoy having Moth around
the house.

She did the shopping, some dusting and hoo-
vering, and learned how to make pastry, surprising herself with a crisp steak and kidney pie that
Libby, not one for flattery, pronounced terrific.
It was as though she had had a severe illness – the
kind that children in old-fashioned books used to
have – and was now convalescent. She knew that
she couldn't go on like this, but she was grateful
for the chance to recover in her own way.

Then one afternoon the bell rang, and there
on the doorstep was Miss Pearson. Moth looked

at her as though she belonged to another life.

'Well, aren't you going to ask me in? If you won't come to me, I thought perhaps Mahomet had better come to the mountain.'

Moth grinned sheepishly. 'Did you want to see my great-aunt? She's lying down at the moment.'

'No, I've come to see you. I thought it might be easier to have a talk at home, where there's no one to disturb us.'

Moth led her upstairs and into the drawing room, where Miss Pearson perched on the settee and came straight to the point. 'I'm afraid the Royal Ballet School are not going to offer you a place. Their osteopath feels that your feet aren't strong enough to take the strain of a career in classical ballet. I think you already knew that, didn't you?'

'Yes,' Moth agreed miserably. She had known, and yet . . .

'I'm sorry, because I know you must be very disappointed and you're one of the most promising dancers we've had in a long time. Technique has never been your strong point – you feel too much to have a reliable technique – but you're blessed with an unusual, creative appreciation of dancing.'

'The others . . .?' Moth wanted to get it over.

'Tom has been offered a place and so has

Libby. Linden has been accepted for the teaching course, but you weren't interested in that, were you?'

'No.' Moth couldn't stop the tears coming . . . Libby, who'd been her rival all along . . . who was so unaffected by life and always got what she wanted . . . Libby had fulfilled Moth's dream and would go on and on . . .

Miss Pearson ignored Moth's tears. 'So what we have to decide now is what you are going to do next, and I've got one idea you might like to consider.'

'I don't want to be a teacher, or do my A levels and go to university,' Moth gulped. 'And I don't want anything more to do with dancing, now that I can't dance.'

'Who said you can't dance?' Miss Pearson didn't sound in the least sympathetic. 'You can go on dancing if you're really determined, and I came round here because I thought that was what you wanted. I didn't know you'd changed your mind.'

'I haven't, but it's been changed for me, hasn't it?'

'My dear Moth, like hundreds of other aspiring dancers you've failed to get into a course that would have qualified you at best to be a classical dancer. What you think of as the lucky ones will get a training that will make them more marketable as classical dancers, but their chance of getting into the company is very remote.

'All the White Lodge students are put in one class, and new recruits to the company usually come from that class; only the odd girl from the other classes stands a ghost of a chance of being picked. You certainly wouldn't have been, because you have neither the technique nor the temperament to stand up to the tough world of the company. Your gifts are only likely to flourish in very different soil.'

Moth didn't understand what she was getting at.

'The best thing you've done so far was that little ballet about the mad girl. You threw yourself into it because you enjoy creating, and I think that's the area we should concentrate on now.'

'But I can't just become a choreographer . . .'

'No, of course not, but you stand a much greater chance in a different atmosphere, somewhere that welcomes ideas, that's closer to the way ballet is going in the future than a major prestige company can afford to be.'

'What sort of a place?'

'A friend of mine who teaches at a school of contemporary dance was impressed by your ballet and asked whether you'd thought of auditioning for them. I told her that you'd set your heart on trying for the Royal, and that you'd have to find out for yourself that you weren't right for them before you'd be prepared to consider anything else.'

'You knew all along that I wouldn't get in,' said Moth accusingly.

'I suspected it, yes, but it didn't seem a tragedy, because I knew there were other things open to you.'

'But not the things I want. I quite like the contemporary dance classes, but not in preference to classical. I . . .'

'I suspect you don't really know much about it. You've been so set on one thing for so long that you've shut your eyes to everything else. If you'd ever seen any of the top contemporary dance companies, I don't think you'd feel I was suggesting some kind of second-class consolation prize Modern dance isn't a poor second, Moth, it's an exciting challenge. The school I had in mind has a teacher who trained at the Martha Graham school and is the only person over here teaching the authentic Graham style. But if you don't want to know about it . . .'

'I do.' The world was right-side-up again. 'It's just that I thought I'd got to give up dancing . . . and I've been trying not to think about it.'

'You give in very easily,' said Miss Pearson dryly. 'And I thought you were a fighter.

There's no place in dancing for anyone who isn't. It's going to be disappointments and setbacks all the way, and you seem to have fallen at the first hurdle. Do you really want to go on?'

Moth didn't know. She'd heard all the talk about disappointments before, and battling against misfortune had always sounded so dramatic. But over the past week misfortune had left her numb and frightened, stumbling around in a paralysing web of depression. She couldn't really say, not with any conviction, yes, I don't care what happens, I can take anything, because she wasn't sure that she could. But she did want to dance.

'Well, think it over.' Miss Pearson's tone was a shade more kindly in response to Moth's obvious distress. 'The auditions aren't until next term, so you've got time to find out about contemporary dance. Go and see some companies if you can, and do some research into Martha Graham. They also have student programmes at the school, if you're interested.'

'If I do apply,' Moth said tentatively, 'would my feet be all right? I mean . . .'

'Well, I'm not a doctor, of course, and the audition will include a thorough medical examination, but I think the main objection to your feet was that the high arch wouldn't take the strain of continuous *pointe* work. Contemporary dance uses different techniques and no *pointe* work, so you should be all right.'

Moth wanted to hug Miss Pearson, and her delight showed.

'Moth, I'm not offering you a place at the school. I can't do that. If you do apply, you'll have to be prepared to be turned down again. You do understand that, don't you?'

Moth nodded.

'Good girl. Well I must be on my way. I've got a class at half-past three and I mustn't be late. See you tomorrow – in class.'

Moth didn't argue.

So Libby has passed, she thought, as she came slowly up the stairs after Miss Pearson had gone. She knows where she's going for the next couple of years, whereas I . . .

She heard her great-aunt calling from the bedroom.

'I dropped off, and then I thought I heard the door bang. Is Libby home already? Is it time for tea?'

'No, not yet. I shut the door and I'm sorry I woke you up.' Moth didn't want to talk about Miss Pearson yet, not until she'd adjusted to her change of direction.

'Libby won't be home for another hour at least, so I thought I might go round to the library. Would you like me to change your book?'

'Please. I had a card this morning to say it's my turn for that new thriller, and I'd love to settle down with a nice murder this evening.'

Moth smiled. Her great-aunt's voracious appetite for a good murder was a family joke. She took the card and bounced down the stairs, suddenly feeling restless and tingling with energy. She had her own reason for going to the library: she wanted to see whether they had any books on Martha Graham – the name itself seemed a good omen – and contemporary dance.

# 14

## *All in the Stars*

It was no good Moth going to bed early, because she knew she wouldn't sleep. However hard she tried – and trying to relax seemed rather a contradiction – she couldn't seem to unwind, or stop thinking about tomorrow.

Tomorrow was the day of the audition for the school of contemporary dance.

The last weeks had been full of worrying days, and yet the GCSEs, important though everyone said they were, had meant little to Moth in comparison. As a result, she had probably done quite well, because the sudden fear that made her adrenalin spurt had come only at the last minute, when she saw the paper. The Cecchetti exam didn't matter much either, because although it would be nice to end her classical dancing with a flourish, dancing might not matter at all after tomorrow.

She was tempted to run through her set dance again, and checked for the hundredth time that the tape of the Poulenc flute music was with her shoes and leotard. Jane, who'd been given the tape by a well-meaning aunt who was a great fan of James Galway, had swapped the flute concertos for Moth's old *Nutcracker*. The Poulenc was cool, haunting, wistful music, the voice of a woodland nymph or a water sprite, and when Miss Pearson had asked her to do something for the end of term show – positively my last appearance, Moth thought – Moth had suggested a solo dance that had no theme beyond unfolding and interpreting the music.

'Good idea,' said Miss Pearson, 'and you can use it for your audition too. I was going to suggest you did part of the mad woman dance, but something new would be much better.'

It was done, and going over it again would only spoil the freshness. She must leave well alone.

'I think I'll go out for a walk. Just round the block,' she added, to reassure her great-aunt. 'I feel as though I've got itchy blood in my veins. You know that feeling.'

Great-Aunt Marion looked vaguely troubled; she had become even more cautious since her accident.

'I'll be all right. I'm not going anywhere

dangerous or lonely, and there'll be plenty of people about on such a lovely evening.'

It was high summer and the air smelled of grass. In front gardens mowers rattled back and forth across lawns too modest for Flymos, and men armed with deafening high-powered cutters worked off their frustrations on small hedges. The sun had set, but the sky was still flushed with heat and the light stood still. Moth remembered playing in the garden on similar evenings when she was small, and felt as though she could reach back through time and touch the child she had been.

Her favourite walk was past a house with a high-walled garden that roused her curiosity. The weathered planks of the garden door had parted with age, and Moth poked at them, trying to increase the gap. She was so absorbed in peering through, that she ignored the sound of footsteps until hands fixed her to the door and a voice said teasingly: 'Guess who?'

It was Daniel. Moth hadn't seen him for ages, and according to Ruth he'd been in a foul mood, driving himself hard for his scholarship.

'What's so intriguing about the view?' Daniel pressed his eye to the crack, which was wider high up.

Moth was afraid that he would say something

crushing if she told him that she found secret gardens intriguing.

'I can see a statue,' he said. 'Makes you want to see more. Did you ever read *The Secret Garden* when you were little?'

'Yes.'

'With the Robinson illustrations?'

'Are they the old-fashioned ones with lots of mauve and grey and brown?'

'That's right. It was one of my mother's favourite books, so we got it read to us whenever we were ill. Well, what have you been doing?'

'Exams mostly. Now they're all over, there's nothing much left to do at school. It's as if we'd suddenly outgrown it. How about you?'

They had begun to walk along together, and Moth realised it was the first time she had been on her own with Daniel.

'Exams of a sort too, but it's all over now, at least for the time being. I've got my scholarship and I'm going to study in Moscow.'

'You're going away!' Moth couldn't hide her dismay.

'For a year at first, maybe longer. It depends how I get on.'

'Are you scared? I think I would be.'

'If you were offered a place at the Kirov? I thought Russia was the great Mecca of dancers.

Isn't the Kirov, or is it the Bolshoi, supposed to be the greatest company in the world?'

'I think it's the Kirov. They produced all the famous dancers we know about, like Nureyev and Makarova. But aren't you scared of going somewhere where you don't speak the language?'

'Not really. I've been trying to learn a little Russian, to go with my reasonable French and not very good German. Travel's a way of life for concert pianists. If I make it, I'll probably spend my life flying all over the world – and I do so hate flying.'

'Where are we going?' Moth had the feeling that their walk had some definite goal.

'It's a place I come to when I want to unwind after practising. You could say it's my secret garden, though it's not private. It's a public park, but not many people come here because I don't think they know about it. I came across it one day when I was feeling very depressed, and it so cheered me up that I decided it was my lucky place.'

The park must once have been part of a large old garden that had been swallowed up by the surrounding houses. The paths wound between tangles of pale scented roses, not at all like the gaudy ones with no perfume that usually grew in park beds; in the centre was a lawn of grass so well-kept that it looked as though nobody ever walked on it.

Daniel behaved as though the place belonged to him. He sprawled on the grass while Moth sat down beside him and then lay back and looked up at the tall sky. There were still splashes of fiery gold and it seemed as though it would never get dark.

'The Land of the Midnight Sun,' said Daniel, echoing her thoughts. 'I wonder where we'll be this time next year?'

'I shall only know after tomorrow,' said Moth dramatically. 'My whole future will be decided then.'

'Sounds drastic. What happens tomorrow?'

'My audition. If I don't get accepted, I won't be dancing any more.'

'Oh, you'll get in – if you dance like you did at that show.'

'Do you think so?' Moth was thrilled by Daniel's casual praise.

'You will if you're meant to dance. That's what I told myself at my audition. If I'm meant to go on, I shall get the scholarship. If I don't, then it's a sign that I shan't ever be a pianist. And I got it.'

'But supposing you hadn't?'

'I'd have accepted that I wasn't meant to go to Moscow and looked around for what else was on offer. I believe you get what you're meant to have, and if this school is the right place for you, you'll get in. It's as simple as that.'

Moth looked up at Daniel and envied his self-assurance. She did feel she was meant to dance, and yet . . .

'My father believes it. He's never pretended that the plan was something you could under-stand. It could mean you get killed or die young . . . and it doesn't work unless you co-operate. I mean you don't pass exams without doing any work . . . But he says that things don't happen by chance, that the people you meet are often there, at that moment in life, because it's the right moment for you to meet them. I like the idea that I may be set on a collision course with someone I don't know yet, but who may change my life.'

'Like it's all in the stars.'

'I suppose so. Like this evening. I don't often go down that road, do you?'

'I don't often go out for a walk at night,' Moth admitted.

'Well there you are. We were meant to meet.'

They looked at each other, uncertain of where they had arrived, or how to go on. Daniel jumped up, suddenly embarrassed, and began to do cartwheels across the lawn.

Moth watched him, excited, disappointed,

wishing she wasn't shy. Then she wheeled across the grass in his wake, spinning joyfully into a world upside down.

'Home,' called Daniel, running down the street, and only when Moth had nearly caught him did he turn, in mid-flight, and hold out his hand.

# 15

## Casting Vote

The school was a warren of studios, music rooms and offices, linked by chipped stone steps and a brightly-painted iron fire-escape. Someone with a sense of humour had been let loose with a paintbrush and had turned the pipes of the old building into cheerful ribbons of colour. Moth felt they proclaimed that the spirit of the place was the complete opposite of institutional sludge green.

Not that there was much time to look round and take in the atmosphere. Once assembled, the candidates for the audition were told to change and warm up. Moth saw she was by far the youngest. Only one other girl, whose copper hair clashed with her cherry red leotard, seemed to be about Moth's age.

'Right, now we're starting early' – the speaker was a pleasant but determined-looking woman –

'because we've got a lot to get through. First we want you to do a simple ballet class, and then a modern dance class. This will give us a chance to see how you move and how adaptable you are. We know some of you are more experienced than others, and we shall be making allowances for this. Then we shall ask some of you to drop out – either because we don't think you're right for this kind of training, or because you're not ready for it yet. The others will have an interview with the principal and our counsellor, and be examined by the osteopath. This afternoon there'll be a class to test your interpretative ability, and then you'll do your solos. Any questions?'

Nobody had. Uncertain and a trifle apprehensive, they crowded protectively together as they were shown into a studio.

Moth had no trouble with the sequences they were asked to do. She was used to memorising far more elaborate *enchainements*, and the feeling that the steps were well within her grasp steadied and reassured her. The staff watched intently, making rapid squiggles on their clipboards, and she guessed that it was the simple things that were the real giveaway. Just standing still was a test of grace, relaxation and poise, and the curve of an arm said volumes to an experienced teacher.

She had a chance to assess her rivals when each row danced separately. Some were laughably gauche, like the two lanky boys who kept colliding with each other as though they were doing a comedy routine. But she was impressed by a fair-haired boy with a grave expression and the spring of a jack-in-a-box, who danced as though his life depended on it.

They moved to a bigger studio for the modern dance class. Windows of sunlight rippled across the floor; in the background Moth could hear the various rhythms of pianos all over the building, accompanying individuals, classes and possibly the company itself.

An alarming little woman with grey hair cut in an uncompromising fringe commanded them to get rid of any socks or ankle-warmers. Garbage, she called them. Being aware of their bare feet on the ground was important, a deliberate contrast to classical ballet, which was always trying to fly away from the earth. Modern dance was about having your feet on the ground.

Instead of standing at the barre, they did their exercises sitting down, bending, stretching, swivelling, and sliding their feet and legs across the floor. The movements stressed the breathing rhythms of contraction and release, pulling in the muscles of the diaphragm, using dramatic, angular thrusts so that at times it was as though they were fighting the floor. The teacher's voice was gentle, but her words were forceful. 'Sneak in a change of leg,' she suggested; 'pull the room with you.'

Then they had to walk slowly across the room, turn on tiptoe, raise their arms, and race from corner to corner in a headlong dash. Some ran recklessly, as though speed was what mattered; others spanned the room with graceful *jetés* that revealed some classical training.

The teachers made more notes, whispering among themselves and occasionally laughing at some private joke.

Sweat ran in tears down the fair boy's face; the girl in cherry red had a face to match. Moth felt exhausted and exhilarated. Modern dance at the Fortune was never like this: harsh, urgent and exciting.

Then it was over, and the staff swept off to compare notes over coffee. Their comments were frank. 'That girl's hopeless: the hips of an elephant and bad posture. That boy in purple was just sleeping his way through. His body was all right, but he didn't seem to be inside it. Looked like an empty space.'

The list was gradually whittled down: flair, warmth, energy were recognised, tension, laziness, displeasing proportions rejected. There was a heated argument over a girl suspected of being neurotic. 'I know that type,' said one teacher darkly. 'If she comes here, I'm not having her in my class.' No one felt strongly enough to insist, so the girl was crossed off and the secretary despatched to divide the wheat from the chaff.

Moth wasn't surprised to be chosen. Few of the others, she gathered, had had full-time training, and it showed. They talked in shy whispers as they sat outside the principal's study. One boy had never been to London before and had come with his elder sister, who sat patiently in the corridor, too scared to venture outside until it was time to go home. Moth learned with a pang that one girl had been at White Lodge until she outgrew the Royal shape. She didn't seem to mind much and was disappointingly ordinary: she wanted to go on dancing because she couldn't think of anything else to do. Moth would like to have talked to the fair boy, but he was shut away in an intense world of his own.

The principal was a surprise. Moth had thought he might be a retired dancer, though she didn't recognise his name, but the young man confronting her had plainly not had time to retire from anything.

'I see you've been dancing full-time since you were eleven,' he said, reading her application form, 'so I don't need to warn you about the hard work involved. What I'd like to know, is why you want to switch to modern dance after all your classical training?' He looked friendly enough, but Moth sensed that he would see through any unconvincing reasons. It was safer to tell the truth.

'I wanted to be a classical dancer,' she admitted, 'but my feet aren't strong enough for *pointe* work. I want to go on dancing, more than anything in the world, so my teacher suggested modern dance.'

'I see.' He was making notes. 'And how do you like changing direction? Have you seen any modern dance companies?'

Moth nodded. 'I saw a couple at Sadler's Wells, and I came to a student programme here.'

'And what did you make of it? Can you tell me anything you specially liked?'

Moth couldn't get it all together. Names seemed tantalisingly beyond her reach. She remembered dancers mimicking animals, a ballet about Mary and an angel, a group of students groping their way through unfamiliar, discordant music.

'I – I can't remember any names, but I liked what I saw because it was rather like what I was trying to do in a ballet I made up for our end-of-term show. The ones I saw were more complicated, more like poems . . .' Moth tailed off, unable to put into words what she had felt about dancing that spoke a new, bewildering language that she didn't, as yet, understand.

The principal smiled. 'A poem is a good comparison,' he said, 'and you'd certainly get a chance to create your own ballets, as we have a choreography class that would welcome a keen recruit. Now what about the practicalities? If you come to us next year, you'll be only sixteen; most of our students are quite a lot older. Do you think you'll be able to cope?'

Moth wasn't sure what he was getting at. 'I'm used to being away from home,' she said, anxious to underline her independence, 'and I could go on living with my great-aunt, like I do now.'

'Well that would certainly be useful, as accommodation is one of our greatest problems. That and money. You'll be asking your local authority for a grant, I take it?'

'Yes.' The fact that if she was offered a place she would get a grant, had been Miss Pearson's trump card in persuading Moth's parents that modern dance was worthwhile. Mr Graham had been far from convinced; like Mrs Blundell-Smith, he had an uneasy feeling that anything 'modern' was dangerous. He'd seen some modern dancing on television, and it seemed to involve 'a lot of rolling round on the floor'.

'Good.' The principal went on writing. 'Well, Jennifer, I'd like you to have a talk with our counsellor, who will outline some of the problems you may not have thought of, and then the osteopath will have a look at you. I'll be seeing you again this afternoon. Could you ask the next person to come in, please.'

He gave nothing away, and Moth left the room wondering whether she had impressed him. She had the feeling he knew exactly what he was looking for.

They had been told to bring sandwiches for lunch and were left alone to eat them. At first they munched in silence, but then someone mentioned a summer school – 'Haven't I seen you somewhere before?' – and suddenly everyone was swapping experiences of movement classes, mime, dance composition, doing tap, jazz and ballroom, being in panto, dancing at workshops and festivals.

Janet, the cherry-red girl, danced evenings and weekends. She was game for anything, and told Moth that if she didn't get in, she'd try nursing or hairdressing, as she loved being with people. The fair-haired boy turned out to be at a college in Wales where he taught movement and played the clarinet, while another boy had been working on a kibbutz and had picked up dancing from his girlfriend.

Moth didn't mention the Fortune. It seemed

dull just to have been at school, and she saw
how much her life would have to change for her
to catch up with older students. As the counsellor had explained in their talk, she wouldn't just
be taking on more dancing, but the problems of
adult life.

'And it's tough here. You come in for a lot of
criticism at first, and you have to be able to
separate criticism of you as a dancer from criticism of you as a person. You need a lot of self-
confidence, and we haven't time to keep mop-
ping up tears, which is one reason why we're
very wary of dancers as young as you.'

The osteopath who examined her with an
expertise that missed nothing, was more reassuring. 'At least you're not overweight,' he said
cheerfully when she stood on the scales, 'and
you'd be surprised how many prospective dancers are.'

Moth tried to read his notes, but they were
unintelligible. He didn't seem worried, however,
by her high instep, and she had the feeling that
being considered too young was likely to be
more of a handicap.

The music for the interpretation class was by
Bartok; Moth and the fair boy had heard of him,
but everyone else looked blank. The sequence
was designed to test their imagination and musi-
cality. They had to link arms and dance as a

corps; then they were given a pose and told to express the mood of the music. They had both to relate to the others in their group and devise movements that were individual. Moth took her cue from the fair-haired boy, who saw at once the need to be bold and dramatic.

Then one by one they were summoned to perform their solo, while the others waited outside.

They had all chosen something different, the fair boy dancing like Pan to some oboe solos by Britten, while the girl from White Lodge didn't know what her piece was called.

Moth announced her Poulenc concerto and added that it was a dance without a story. It was hard to suit the mood to the afternoon sunlight when the music suggested early morning or twilight, and she had to shut out the studio and the critical audience. She was in a control room, balancing the music against her awareness of the space to be filled, the demands of the steps, the shape of the dance. Her feeling that she had done well came not from the audience – though they looked as though they had enjoyed it – but from her sense of being in charge. She had conquered her nerves, concentrated, and done her best when it mattered most.

'Thank you,' said the principal. 'If you want to know the result, give us a ring in the morning.'

\* \* \*

The discussion in the staffroom was held over until they had had tea. Audition days were famous for being thirsty work.

The fair boy chose himself. Everyone agreed he was dedicated, gifted, and deserved a special scholarship. The boy from the kibbutz, though lacking personality, had a good trainable body, and they were short of men. The osteopath eliminated nearly everyone else because of restricted movements, pelvic shifts, unstable ankles and past injuries, but even he couldn't find much wrong with cherry-red Janet.

'That girl's a honey. She's got such zip, energy and sparkle. We must have her.'

Then they came to Jennifer Graham.

'Nice little mover, well trained, obviously keen, but . . .'

'Too young. How about asking her to come back next year?'

'She looks too sensitive. She'll never stand up to our lot.'

'She's keen on choreography.' This was Miss Pearson's friend. 'Just for once, can't I have someone who actually wants to do it before she gets here.'

'She could be neurotic. Remember Veronica . . .' There were sighs all round and calls for another cup of tea. Everyone remembered Veronica all too clearly.

'Let's vote. Those in favour?'

It was a tie.

'Come on, Richard. You've got the casting vote. What did you make of her?'

The principal looked at his notes. 'I agree she looks rather sensitive and she is very young. I would have misgivings if she was going to be on her own, but she could be company for Janet, who will also be only sixteen. I think they might be good for each other. I'm influenced too by the fact that she'll be living with a relative, so there'll be someone in the background to keep an eye on her.

'Most of the kids we've seen today see dancing as no more than self-expression, something that draws attention to themselves, but she impressed me as caring about dancing for its own sake. She'd actually bothered to go and see the company!

'I may be making a mistake, for which I shall of course take the blame' – there were teasing cries of 'Mind you do!' – 'but I think we should stick out our necks and give Jennifer Graham a chance.'

'So, that makes four for next year. Four out of fifteen. That's not bad for a hard day's work. And now, please, can we all go home.'

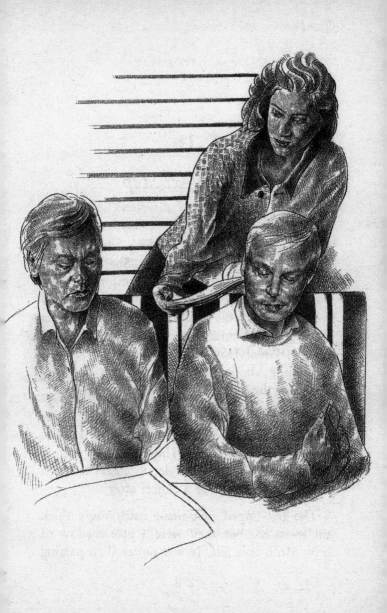

# 16

## *The Next Step*

Moth found the blue leather diary when she was doing her end-of-term packing. She had meant to keep a close record of such an important year, but alas there were lots of gaps, and the last few weeks, some of the busiest and most eventful in her life, were blank. There wasn't even an entry for the Great Day, but at least she could do something about that. She found a pen and turned to the middle of June.

27 June. Rang up the school. It was agony holding on while the secretary checked. Then she told me I'd got in. They would be writing to confirm it, and send details etc. A frabjous day! I'm going to be a dancer after all!!!!

The felt-tipped pen made satisfyingly thick exclamations, but they were a pale shadow of how Moth had felt. It was better than passing exams, better than the trophy she'd won at a festival. She had started out like hundreds of other girls to be a dancer, and she had made it.

No, that wasn't quite true, because there was still a long uncertain way to go, as her father had been quick to point out. He was profoundly suspicious of modern dance, and it had taken the combined forces of Miss Lambert, Miss Pearson and the principal of the school to persuade him that it was a worthwhile career.

'Whatever they say,' he insisted afterwards, 'you could be wasting your grant on three years that lead nowhere. Then it's no good changing your mind and wishing you'd gone to university instead, because there'll be no money for that.'

Moth brandished a list of jobs found by the school's most recent graduates, and pointed out that most of them seemed to have got jobs within six months of graduating. Her father, however, was not impressed by companies he'd never heard of, and Moth hoped he wouldn't notice that one of them was based in Venezuela. He saw getting a job, she realised, as the point of the whole thing. Being creative was a waste of time, or just a nice hobby, if you couldn't earn a living from it.

She flicked through the diary, blushing at an entry about Dan, and then remembered that she was supposed to have finished her packing by the time her mother got back. The family had come up to London for the end-of-term show, and her mother had taken Toby and Lyn shopping while her father sunned himself at Lords. After tea they were driving home, and the summer holidays yawned like a boring interval before Moth could get on with her life.

She looked round to see if there was anything else she ought to take home. She would need most of her dance things next term, but the odd leotard might be useful. She would need to practise, perhaps at some local class – if they didn't all shut down for the summer. She would like to have gone to another summer school, but she knew her father would go through the roof if she so much as breathed of any more expense.

She glanced at her books and was annoyed to see that she still had a biography of Martha Graham that belonged to the library. Her great-aunt would take it back for her, but she did have time to return it herself.

She bounced down the stairs, revelling in the feeling that she was free to please herself. Libby was out somewhere, perhaps with Tom. She was flying home tomorrow, but would be back with Great-Aunt Marion in the autumn. The idea of her branching out in flat-sharing had been firmly squashed, but Libby had hinted to Moth that they might be glad to get rid of her before long.

'I'm going to find Hyde,' she promised, 'and no one's going to stop me.'

Well, I'm certainly not, thought Moth. And I'm not going to cover up for you either. We shall go our own ways at last.

Her great-aunt was having her afternoon rest, so Moth shut the front door very quietly. She decided to go to the library by way of the Fishers' house, just in case Daniel happened to be around.

Ruth was going back to the Fortune for another year to do her A levels, and was furious at being left behind. Dr Fisher had agreed to drama school, providing she got a couple of A levels first, and she had joined a youth theatre and was going to spend part of the holidays touring.

Daniel was off to Moscow in the autumn. Moth wanted to see him before he went, and was in two minds about whether to remind him about the Proms. She had thought of writing to him, say, in a light-hearted style that implied she thought the whole thing was a joke, but ... Would he be annoyed, or flattered, or perhaps despise her for being so obvious? It was surely up to him to pursue her, and yet if he did phone, her great-aunt would explain that she'd gone home, and he wouldn't realise that she could come back, would come back, if he wanted to see her. It was all right for Libby to run after Hyde because that was her style, but Moth found herself in strange territory where she was uncertain what to do next.

Her thoughts were interrupted by a man's voice that was unexpected but somehow familiar.

'It *is* Moth, isn't it?'

It was too hot for the college scarf that had been an essential part of his appearance, but the young man in front of her still looked indefinably like a student. Just for a moment, she couldn't think who he was, and then . . .

'Robert!'

'Right in one. I thought I recognised you, but I wasn't sure. You were a mere child last time I saw you, but now . . .'

His expression was openly admiring.

'That was years ago. I haven't seen you since that night we went to Covent Garden, and you wanted to meet Marina Guest.' She remembered, too late, that Robert had been in love with Marina and resented not having the money to take her out. She wondered if he was still interested in her.

'That must have been before I finished my book, which did actually get published, though hardly anyone noticed it. I meant to get in touch again, but I've been in the States on a research fellowship. So what have you been doing with yourself? Are you dancing at the Garden yet?'

'No. I've had to give up classical ballet, but I've changed to modern dance and I'm starting a three-year course at a school of contemporary dance in the autumn.'

'Good for you. So you'll be around next year. We must go to the ballet again, or perhaps you'd prefer a film or a play.'

'I won't be back until the autumn.' Moth wasn't sure how serious the suggestion was, but she sensed that Robert now saw her in a different light.

'It's a date. Remember, I've got a weakness for beautiful dancers,' he said teasingly.

Moth grinned – and then saw from his eyes that he wasn't entirely joking.

'Look, I must go, because I'm due somewhere at four. I'll give you a buzz in September.'

'Bye.' Moth made it sound casual, but that wasn't the way she felt. Robert, who must be years older than she was, wanted to take her out! The idea was disconcerting.

All the way to the library she tried to work out what had changed, and then as she came up the steps she suddenly saw herself reflected in one of the glass doors, and stopped in surprise.

She was looking at a girl in jeans and a T-shirt with long straight brown hair swept back in a pony tail. The girl had a good figure, with a small waist and slim hips, and a certain careless grace. Moth considered her as though she were a stranger, and saw that she was a girl who would be competing with hundreds of other girls to be thought attractive, worth taking out, worth kissing . . .

I shall write to Daniel, she decided. And if he doesn't want to take me out, it doesn't matter, because Robert will, and in time there will be others. She remembered the fair boy at the audition, and wondered whether she would see him again.

'You're Moth Graham,' she told the girl, 'and you're coming back to London to be a dancer.'

The girl looked back at her, a Moth who was older and self-assured, and this girl had the world at her feet.

## Homecoming by Cynthia Voigt
**£3.50**

Dicey made her announcement to James, Sammy and Maybeth: "We're going to have to walk all the way to Bridgeport." But they had no money and the whole world was arranged for people who had money – or rather, for adults who had money. The world was arranged against kids. Well, she could handle it. She'd have to. Somehow.

## Dicey's Song by Cynthia Voigt
**£3.50**

Still troubled about her mother, and anxious about the three younger children, Dicey seems to have no time for growing up – until an incident at school shows her what to do.

## A Solitary Blue by Cynthia Voigt
**£3.50**

Jeff has always been a loner, ever since his mother walked out, leaving him with his taciturn and distant father. Then his mother invites him to Charleston. For one glorious summer, Jeff is happy, before his dreams are shattered.

## The Runner by Cynthia Voigt
**£3.50**

Bullet Tillerman has little interest in anyone or anything except running. But this is the 1960s, and with racial war at home and the Vietnam War abroad, Bullet's beliefs have to change, particularly when he's asked to coach a new black runner at the school.

## Voyage by Adèle Geras
### £1.95
Rain is falling as the ship steams away from the docks. On deck, Mina and the other passengers gaze back at the homelands they are fleeing, and forward to the New World and the future. But does America even exist? And will they ever reach it?

## The Fantora Family Files by Adèle Geras
### £2.50
Ozzy the cat, narrator and keeper of the Files, tells the stories of Filomena, who can tell the future from wool, Francesca, who can create weather to order, and many others in the strange Fantora family.

## The Silver Crown by Robert O'Brien
### £3.50
Ellen had known all along she was a queen, and the silver crown she found on her pillow only went to prove it. Proudly wearing her new present, she tiptoed out for an early morning walk that was to lead her into the realms of deepest danger. Was it the crown they were after – or her?

## The Phantom Tollbooth by Norton Juster
### £3.50
Miserable Milo flopped down in his chair and caught sight of the giant package. "One genuine turnpike tollbooth" reads the note attached, and, for want of something better to do, Milo jumps into the car and journeys through a land in which words and numbers rudely defy the dictates of order and sense.

## Hard and Fast by Linda Newbery
### £3.99

When Melanie organises a sponsored fast at school, she
has no idea of the effect it will have on her friends.
Each of the main characters discovers something about
themselves, so that by the end of the story rather more
than funds for the starving has been achieved.

With strong characterisation and excellent dialogue,
Linda Newbery's novel has both sensitivity and style.

## Run with the Hare by Linda Newbery
### £3.50

A sensitive and authentic novel exploring the workings
of an animal rights group, through the eyes of Elaine, a
sixth-form pupil. Elaine becomes involved with the
group through her more forceful friend Kate, and soon
becomes involved with Mark, an Adult Education
student and one of the more sophisticated members of
the group. Elaine finds herself painting slogans and
sabotaging a fox hunt. Then she and her friends
uncover a dog fighting ring – and things turn very
nasty.

## A Summer to Die
## by Lois Lowry
**£2.99**

Having a sister who is blonde and pretty and popular can be tricky if you're like Meg – serious, hardworking and, well, plain. But when Molly becomes critically ill, Meg has to face up to something much worse than jealousy.

## Number the Stars
## by Lois Lowry
(Newbery Award Winner 1990)
**£2.99**

Copenhagen, 1943. Annemarie carries on her normal life under the shadow of the Nazis – until they begin their campaign to "relocate" the Jews of Denmark. Annemarie's best friend Ellen is a Jew, and Annemarie is called upon to help Ellen and many others escape across the sea.

## Switcharound
## by Lois Lowry
**£3.50**

Caroline and JP are not thrilled at the thought of spending the summer with their father. On a scale of 1 to 10, with nuclear war as 10, JP gives it 8, Caroline 9. But things are never quite as bad as they seem...or are they?

## The Coal House by Andrew Taylor
### £2.50

Alison, having moved north, is full of resentment at leaving behind friends and all she knows. But in the overgrown garden of the Coal House she meets two very different people. Gradually she learns about the House's past owners and the tragedy in their lives which in turn affect her own life.

## The Girls' Gang by Rose Impey
### £2.75

Sandra, Jane, Cheryl, Jo and Louise are sick and tired of being teased and pushed about by Ralph Raven and the other boys, but they soon realise that if they stick together in a gang girls can do anything boys can do, only better.

## The Woods at the End of Autumn Street by Lois Lowry
### £1.95

Everything is new and strange to Liz, and she is glad to find an ally in Charles when she moves to her grandfather's house. But their attempts to make sense of a confusing and sometimes cruel adult world come to a violent, tragic end.

## Z for Zachariah by Robert O'Brien
### £2.99

After the nuclear holocaust – what? Sixteen-year-old Anne, alone in an isolated valley, believes that she is the sole survivor of the atomic war that has devastated the surrounding land. The relief she feels when a scientist arrives gradually turns to fear when she learns about his sinister past.

### The Indian in the Cupboard
### by Lynne Reid Banks

When Omri is given a toy Indian and a small cupboard for his birthday, it seems natural to keep the Indian safely in the cupboard. And when, amazingly, the little man comes to life, Omri is thrilled at the thought of all the wonderful games they can play. It isn't long, though, before he realises that being responsible for another human being, no matter how small, is no laughing matter...

### Return of the Indian by Lynne Reid Banks

Just over a year after Omri and his best friend, Patrick, have renounced the alarming power of bringing their model people to life, the boys find the temptation quite irresistible. But this time, the boys discover the added excitement of transporting themselves to a different place and time, with dangerous results.

### The Secret of the Indian
### by Lynne Reid Banks

After a terrible battle, many of Little Bull's warriors are wounded. Omri must get them medical help, but he must also protect the secret of the Indian. When Patrick goes back in time to the Wild West and falls into terrible danger, keeping the secret safe becomes even more difficult for Omri.

**All at £3.99**

## The Fairy Rebel by Lynne Reid Banks

Jan is moping in the garden when Tiki is accidentally "earthed" on her big toe. Being "earthed" for a fairy means that she can be seen, and Tiki has just broken one of the most important fairy rules. Another important rule is never to give humans magic favours, but when Tiki hears Jan's very special wish, she is determined to help, risking the Fairy Queen's fury with frightening results.

## The Farthest-Away Mountain
## by Lynne Reid Banks

From Dakin's bedroom window, the farthest-away mountain looks quite close. She can see the peak with its multi-coloured snow clearly, just beyond the pine wood. No one can tell her why the snow isn't white, because no one has ever been there; for though the mountain looks close, however far you travel it never gets any closer. Then one morning, Dakin is woken by a voice calling, summoning her to fight the evil on the mountain and set it free...

## I, Houdini by Lynne Reid Banks

Houdini is no ordinary hamster. Like his namesake, he was born with quite exceptional talents for getting out of cages. He chews, wriggles or squeezes his way out of every cage his adoring people try to confine him to, strewing chaos, havoc and flood behind him and surviving fearful dangers.

**All at £2.99**

# Order Form

To order direct from the publishers, just make a list of the titles you want and fill in the form below:

Name ...........................................................................

Address .......................................................................

.......................................................................................

.......................................................................................

Send to: Dept 6, HarperCollins Publishers Ltd, Westerhill Road, Bishopbriggs, Glasgow G64 2QT.

Please enclose a cheque or postal order to the value of the cover price, plus:

**UK & BFPO**: Add £1.00 for the first book, and 25p per copy for each addition book ordered.

**Overseas and Eire**: Add £2.95 service charge. Books will be sent by surface mail but quotes for airmail despatch will be given on request.

A 24-hour telephone ordering service is avail-able to Visa and Access card holders: 041-772 2281